KU-444-257

SOUL FOOD

NEIL ASTLEY is editor of Bloodaxe Books, which he founded in 1978, and was given a D.Litt by Newcastle University in 1995 for his pioneering work. He has edited over 800 poetry books and published several anthologies, including *Poetry with an Edge* (1988/1995), *Staying Alive: real poems for unreal times* (2002/2003 USA), *Pleased to See Me: 69 Very Sexy Poems* (2002), *Do Not Go Gentle: poems for funerals* (2003), *Being Alive: the sequel to 'Staying Alive'* (2004), *Passionfood: 100 Love Poems* (2005) and *Earth Shattering: ecopoems* (2007), as well as two poetry collections, *Darwin Survivor* (1988) and *Biting My Tongue* (1995), and two novels, *The End of My Tether* (2002/2003) (shortlisted for the Whitbread First Novel Award), and *The Sheep Who Changed the World* (2005). He lives in Northumberland's Tarset valley.

PAMELA ROBERTSON-PEARCE is an artist and filmmaker. Her films include *IMAGO: Meret Oppenheim* (1996), on the artist who made the fur-lined teacup, and *Gifted Beauty* (2000), about Surrealist women artists including Leonora Carrington and Remedios Varo. *IMAGO: Meret Oppenheim* won several awards, including the Swiss Film Board's Prize for Outstanding Quality and the Gold Apple Award at the National Educational Film and Video Festival in America. She has shown her work in solo exhibitions in New York and Provincetown (Cape Cod), and in various group shows in the US and Europe. Born in Stockholm, she grew up in Sweden, Spain and England, and then for over 20 years lived mostly in America – also working in Switzerland, Norway and Albania – before moving to Northumberland.

SOUL FOOD

NOURISHING POEMS
FOR STARVED MINDS

EDITED BY NEIL ASTLEY
& PAMELA ROBERTSON-PEARCE

BLOODAXE BOOKS

Selection copyright © 2007 Neil Astley & Pamela Robertson-Pearce.

Copyright of poems rests with authors and other rights holders cited on pages 156-59 which constitute an extension of this copyright page.

ISBN: 978 1 85224 766 9

First published 2007 by
Bloodaxe Books Ltd,
Highgreen,
Tarset,
Northumberland NE48 1RP.

www.bloodaxebooks.com
For further information about Bloodaxe titles
please visit our website or write to
the above address for a catalogue.

ᴬᴿᵀˢ ᶜᴼᵁₙ꜀ᵢₗ Bloodaxe Books Ltd acknowledges
the financial assistance of
ₑₙ_GLAₙᴰ Arts Council England, North East.

LEGAL NOTICE

All rights reserved. No part of this book may be reproduced, stored in a retrieval system, or transmitted in any form, or by any means, electronic, mechanical, photocopying, recording or otherwise, without prior written permission from the copyright holders listed on pages 156-59. Bloodaxe Books Ltd only controls publication rights to poems from its own publications and does *not* control rights to most of the poems published in this anthology.

For Noah

Printed in Great Britain by Bell & Bain Limited, Glasgow, Scotland.

Contents

3. THE JOURNEY

4. KNOWING YOURSELF

5. BELIEVING BODY AND SOUL

9. INNER LIGHT

'To be great, be whole...'

FERNANDO PESSOA

translated from the Portuguese
by RICHARD ZENITH

To be great, be whole: don't exaggerate
        Or leave out any part of you.
Be complete in each thing. Put all you are
        Into the least of your acts.
So too in each lake, with its lofty life,
        The whole moon shines.

[14 February 1933]

Auguries of Innocence

WILLIAM BLAKE

To see a world in a grain of sand
And a heaven in a wild flower,
Hold infinity in the palm of your hand
And eternity in an hour.

The Guest House

RUMI

translated from the Persian
by COLEMAN BARKS
with JOHN MOYNE

This being human is a guesthouse.
Every morning a new arrival.

A joy, a depression, a meanness,
some momentary awareness comes
as an unexpected visitor.

Welcome and entertain them all!
Even if they're a crowd of sorrows,
who violently sweep your house
empty of its furniture,
still, treat each guest honorably.
He may be clearing you out
for some new delight.

The dark thought, the shame, the malice,
meet them at the door laughing,
and invite them in.

Be grateful for whoever comes,
because each has been sent
as a guide from beyond.

When the Shoe Fits

CHUANG-TZU

translated from the Chinese
by THOMAS MERTON

Ch'ui the draftsman
Could draw more perfect circles freehand
Than with a compass.

His fingers brought forth
Spontaneous forms from nowhere. His mind
Was meanwhile free and without concern
With what he was doing.

No application was needed
His mind was perfectly simple
And knew no obstacle.

So, when the shoe fits
The foot is forgotten,
When the belt fits
The belly is forgotten,
When the heart is right
"For" and "against" are forgotten.

No drives no compulsions,
No needs, no attractions:
Then your affairs
Are under control.
You are a free man.

Easy is right. Begin right
And you are easy.
Continue easy and you are right.
The right way to go easy
Is to forget the right way
And forget that the going is easy.

Daily Wages

AMRITA PRITAM

*translated from the Punjabi
by* CHARLES BRASCH
with AMRITA PRITAM

In a corner of blue sky
The mill of night whistles,
A white thick smoke
Pours from the moon-chimney.

In dream's many furnaces
Labourer love
Is stoking all the fires

I earn our meeting
Holding you for a while,
My day's wages.

I buy my soul's food
Cook and eat it
And set the empty pot in the corner.

I warm my hands at the dying fire
And lying down to rest
Give God thanks.

The mill of night whistles
And from the moon-chimney
Smoke rises, sign of hope.

I eat what I earn
Not yesterday's leftovers,
And leave no grain for tomorrow.

The Boat

KABIR

translated from the Hindi
by ROBERT BLY

The Guest is inside you, and also inside me;
you know the sprout is hidden inside the seed.
We are all struggling; none of us has gone far.
Let your arrogance go, and look around inside.

The blue sky opens out farther and farther,
the daily sense of failure goes away,
the damage I have done to myself fades,
a million suns come forward with light,
when I sit firmly in that world.

I hear bells ringing that no one has shaken;
inside "love" there is more joy than we know of;
rain pours down, although the sky is clear of clouds;
there are whole rivers of light.
The universe is shot through in all parts by a single sort of love.
How hard it is to feel that joy in all our four bodies!

Those who hope to be reasonable about it fail.
The arrogance of reason has separated us from that love.
With the word "reason" you already feel miles away.

How lucky Kabir is, that surrounded by all this joy
he sings inside his own little boat.
His poems amount to one soul meeting another.
These songs are about forgetting dying and loss.
They rise above both coming in and going out.

Buddha in Glory

RAINER MARIA RILKE

translated from the German
by STEPHEN MITCHELL

Center of all centers, core of cores,
almond self-enclosed and growing sweet –
all this universe, to the furthest stars
and beyond them, is your flesh, your fruit.

Now you feel how nothing clings to you;
your vast shell reaches into endless space,
and there the rich, thick fluids rise and flow.
Illuminated in your infinite peace,

a billion stars go spinning through the night,
blazing high above your head.
But *in* you is the presence that
will be, when all the stars are dead.

The Weighing

JANE HIRSHFIELD

The heart's reasons
seen clearly,
even the hardest
will carry
its whip-marks and sadness
and must be forgiven.

As the drought-starved
eland forgives
the drought-starved lion
who finally takes her,
enters willingly then
the life she cannot refuse,
and is lion, is fed,
and does not remember the other.

So few grains of happiness
measured against all the dark
and still the scales balance.

The world asks of us
only the strength we have and we give it.
Then it asks more, and we give it.

Briefly It Enters, and Briefly Speaks

JANE KENYON

I am the blossom pressed in a book,
found again after two hundred years....

I am the maker, the lover, and the keeper....

When the young girl who starves
sits down to a table
she will sit beside me....

I am food on the prisoner's plate....

I am water rushing to the wellhead,
filling the pitcher until it spills....

I am the patient gardener
of the dry and weedy garden....

I am the stone step,
the latch, and the working hinge....

I am the heart contracted by joy...
the longest hair, white
before the rest....

I am there in the basket of fruit
presented to the widow....

I am the musk rose opening
unattended, the fern on the boggy summit....

I am the one whose love
overcomes you, already with you
when you think to call my name....

The Fountain

DENISE LEVERTOV

Don't say, don't say there is no water
to solace the dryness at our hearts.
I have seen

the fountain springing out of the rock wall
and you drinking there. And I too
before your eyes

found footholds and climbed
to drink the cool water.

The woman of that place, shading her eyes,
frowned as she watched – but not because
she grudged the water,

only because she was waiting
to see we drank our fill and were
refreshed.

Don't say, don't say there is no water.
That fountain is there among its scalloped
green and gray stones,

it is still there and always there
with its quiet song and strange power
to spring in us,
up and out through the rock.

Breaking

WENDELL BERRY

Did I believe I had a clear mind?
It was like the water of a river
flowing shallow over the ice. And now
that the rising water has broken
the ice, I see that what I thought
was the light is part of the dark.

To Know
the Dark

WENDELL BERRY

To go in the dark with a light is to know the light.
To know the dark, go dark. Go without sight,
and find that the dark, too, blooms and sings,
and is traveled by dark feet and dark wings.

In Silence

THOMAS MERTON

Be still
Listen to the stones of the wall.
Be silent, they try
To speak your

Name.
Listen
To the living walls.
Who are you?
Who
Are you? Whose
Silence are you?

Who (be quiet)
Are you (as these stones
Are quiet). Do not
Think of what you are
Still less of
What you may one day be.
Rather
Be what you are (but who?) be
The unthinkable one
You do not know.

O be still, while
You are still alive,
And all things live around you
Speaking (I do not hear)
To your own being,
Speaking by the Unknown
That is in you and in themselves.

'I will try, like them
To be my own silence:
And this is difficult. The whole
World is secretly on fire. The stones
Burn, even the stones
They burn me. How can a man be still or
Listen to all things burning? How can he dare
To sit with them when
All their silence
Is on fire?'

'Everything has been plundered...'

(to Natalya Rykova)

ANNA AKHMATOVA

*translated from the Russian
by* JUDITH HEMSCHEMEYER

[June 1921]

Everything has been plundered, betrayed, sold out,
The wing of black death has flashed,
Everything has been devoured by starving anguish.
Why, then, is it so bright?

The fantastic woods near the town
Wafts the scent of cherry blossoms by day,
At night new constellations shine
In the transparent depths of the skies of July –

And how near the miraculous draws
To the dirty, tumbledown huts...
No one, no one knows what it is,
But for centuries we have longed for it.

Burlap Sack

JANE HIRSHFIELD

A person is full of sorrow
the way a burlap sack is full of stones or sand.
We say, 'Hand me the sack,'
but we get the weight.
Heavier if left out in the rain.
To think that the sand or stones are the self is an error.
To think that grief is the self is an error.
Self carries grief as a pack mule carries the side bags,
being careful between the trees to leave extra room.
The mule is not the load of ropes and nails and axes.
The self is not the miner nor builder nor driver.
What would it be to take the bride
and leave behind the heavy dowry?
To let the thin-ribbed mule browse in tall grasses,
its long ears waggling like the tails of two happy dogs?

Corona

PAUL CELAN

translated from the German
by JOHN FELSTINER

Autumn nibbles its leaf from my hand: we are friends.
We shell time from the nuts and teach it to walk:
time returns into its shell.

In the mirror is Sunday,
in the dream comes sleeping,
the mouth speaks true.

My eye goes down to my lover's loins:
we gaze at each other,
we speak dark things,
we love one another like poppy and memory,
we slumber like wine in the seashells,
like the sun in the moon's blood-jet.

We stand at the window embracing, they watch from the street:
it's time people knew!
It's time the stone consented to bloom,
a heart beat for unrest.
It's time it came time.

It is time.

Archaic Torso of Apollo

RAINER MARIA RILKE

translated from the German by STEPHEN MITCHELL

We cannot know his legendary head
with eyes like ripening fruit. And yet his torso
is still suffused with brilliance from inside,
like a lamp, in which his gaze, now turned to low,

gleams in all its power. Otherwise
the curved breast could not dazzle you so, nor could
a smile run through the placid hips and thighs
to that dark center where procreation flared.

Otherwise this stone would seem defaced
beneath the translucent cascade of the shoulders
and would not glisten like a wild beast's fur:

would not, from all the borders of itself,
burst like a star: for here there is no place
that does not see you. You must change your life.

2. CARPE DIEM

The Summer Day

MARY OLIVER

Who made the world?
Who made the swan, and the black bear?
Who made the grasshopper?
This grasshopper, I mean –
the one who has flung herself out of the grass,
the one who is eating sugar out of my hand,
who is moving her jaws back and forth instead of up and down –
who is gazing around with her enormous and complicated eyes.
Now she lifts her pale forearms and thoroughly washes her face.
Now she snaps her wings open, and floats away.
I don't know exactly what a prayer is.
I do know how to pay attention, how to fall down
into the grass, how to kneel down in the grass,
how to be idle and blessed, how to stroll through the fields,
which is what I have been doing all day.
Tell me, what else should I have done?
Doesn't everything die at last, and too soon?
Tell me, what is it you plan to do
with your one wild and precious life?

Temptation

NINA CASSIAN

translated from the Romanian
by BRENDA WALKER
& ANDREA DELETANT

Call yourself alive? Look, I promise you
that for the first time you'll feel your pores opening
like fish mouths, and you'll actually be able to hear
your blood surging through all those lanes,
and you'll feel light gliding across the cornea
like the train of a dress. For the first time
you'll be aware of gravity
like a thorn in your heel,
and your shoulder blades will ache for want of wings.
Call yourself alive? I promise you
you'll be deafened by dust falling on the furniture,
you'll feel your eyebrows turning to two gashes,
and every memory you have – will begin
at Genesis.

Living

DENISE LEVERTOV

The fire in leaf and grass
so green it seems
each summer the last summer.

The wind blowing, the leaves
shivering in the sun,
each day the last day.

A red salamander
so cold and so
easy to catch, dreamily

moves his delicate feet
and long tail. I hold
my hand open for him to go.

Each minute the last minute.

September Twelfth, 2001

X.J. KENNEDY

Two caught on film who hurtle
from the eighty-second floor,
choosing between a fireball
and to jump holding hands,

aren't us. I wake beside you
stretch, scratch, taste the air,
the incredible joy of coffee
and the morning light.

Alive, we open eyelids
on our pitiful share of time,
we bubbles rising and bursting
in a boiling pot.

Carpe Diem

ROBERT FROST

Age saw two quiet children
Go loving by at twilight,
He knew not whether homeward,
Or outward from the village,
Or (chimes were ringing) churchward.
He waited (they were strangers)
Till they were out of hearing
To bid them both be happy.
'Be happy, happy, happy,
And seize the day of pleasure.'
The age-long theme is Age's.
'Twas Age imposed on poems
Their gather-roses burden
To warn against the danger
That overtaken lovers
From being overflooded
With happiness should have it
And yet not know they have it.
But bid life seize the present?
It lives less in the present
Than in the future always,
And less in both together
Than in the past. The present
Is too much for the senses,
Too crowding, too confusing –
Too present to imagine.

The Good News

THICH NHAT HANH

translated from the Vietnamese
by THICH NHAT HANH
& FRIENDS

[Plum Village, March 1992]

They don't publish
the good news.
The good news is published
by us.
We have a special edition every moment,
and we need you to read it.
The good news is that you are alive,
and the linden tree is still there,
standing firm in the harsh winter.
The good news is that you have wonderful eyes
to touch the blue sky.
The good news is that your child is there before you,
and your arms are available:
hugging is possible.
They only print what is wrong.
Look at each of our special editions.
We always offer the things that are not wrong.
We want you to benefit from them
and help protect them.
The dandelion is there by the sidewalk,
smiling its wondrous smile,
singing the song of eternity.
Listen! You have ears that can hear it.
Bow your head.
Listen to it.
Leave behind the world of sorrow
and preoccupation
and get free.
The latest good news
is that you can do it.

God Speaks to Each of Us

RAINER MARIA RILKE

translated from the German by LEONARD COTTRELL

God speaks to each of us before we are,
Before he's formed us – then, in cloudy speech,
But only then, he speaks these words to each
And silently walks with us from the dark:

Driven by your senses, dare
To the edge of longing. Grow
Like a fire's shadowcasting glare
Behind assembled things, so you can spread
Their shapes on me as clothes.
Don't leave me bare.

Let it all happen to you: beauty and dread.
Simply go – no feeling is too much –
And only this way can we stay in touch.

Near here is the land
That they call Life.
You'll know when you arrive
By how real it is.

Give me your hand.

Chickpea to Cook

RUMI

translated from the Persian by COLEMAN BARKS *with* JOHN MOYNE

A chickpea leaps almost over the rim of the pot
where it's being boiled.

'Why are you doing this to me?'

The cook knocks him down with the ladle.

'Don't you try to jump out.
You think I'm torturing you.
I'm giving you flavor,
so you can mix with spices and rice
and be the lovely vitality of a human being.

Remember when you drank rain in the garden.
That was for this.'

Grace first. Sexual pleasure,
then a boiling new life begins,
and the Friend has something good to eat.

Eventually the chickpea
will say to the cook,
                          'Boil me some more.
Hit me with the skimming spoon.
I can't do this by myself.

I'm like an elephant that dreams of gardens
back in Hindustan and doesn't pay attention
to his driver. You're my cook, my driver,
my way into existence. I love your cooking.'

The cook says,
                    'I was once like you,
fresh from the ground. Then I boiled in time,
and boiled in the body, two fierce boilings.

My animal soul grew powerful.
I controlled it with practices,
and boiled some more, and boiled
once beyond that,
                    and became your teacher.'

How the Rainbow Works

*(for Jean Cook, on learning
of her mother's death)*

AL YOUNG

Mostly we occupy ocular zones, clinging
only to what we think we can see.
We can't see wind or waves of thought,
electrical fields or atoms dancing;
only what they do or make us believe.

Look on all of life as color –
vibratile movement, heart-centered,
from invisibility to the merely visible.
Never mind what happens when one of us dies.
Where are you before you even get born?
Where am I and all the unseeable souls
we love at this moment, or loathed
before birth? Where are we right now?

Everything that ever happened either
never did or always will with variations.
Let's put it another way: Nothing ever
happened that wasn't dreamed, that wasn't
sketched from the start with artful surprises.
Think of the dreamer as God, a painter,
a ham, to be sure, but a divine old master
whose medium is light and who sidesteps
tedium by leaving room both inside and outside
this picture for subjects and scenery to wing it.

Look on death as living color too: the dyeing
of fabric, submersion into a temporary sea,
a spectruming beyond the reach of sensual
range which, like time, is chained to change;
the strange notion that everything we've
ever done or been up until now is past
history, is gone away, is bleached, bereft,
perfect, leaving the scene clean to freshen
with pigment and space and leftover light.

Wild Geese

MARY OLIVER

You do not have to be good.
You do not have to walk on your knees
for a hundred miles through the desert, repenting.
You only have to let the soft animal of your body
    love what it loves.
Tell me about despair, yours, and I will tell you mine.
Meanwhile the world goes on.
Meanwhile the sun and the clear pebbles of the rain
are moving across the landscapes,
over the prairies and the deep trees,
the mountains and the rivers.
Meanwhile the wild geese, high in the clean blue air,
are heading home again.
Whoever you are, no matter how lonely,
the world offers itself to your imagination,
calls to you like the wild geese, harsh and exciting –
over and over announcing your place
in the family of things.

Mother to Son

LANGSTON HUGHES

Well, son, I'll tell you:
Life for me ain't been no crystal stair.
It's had tacks in it,
And splinters,
And boards torn up,
And places with no carpet on the floor —
Bare.
But all the time
I'se been a-climbin' on,
And reachin' landin's,
And turnin' corners,
And sometimes goin' in the dark
Where there ain't been no light.
So, boy, don't you turn back.
Don't you set down on the steps.
'Cause you finds it's kinder hard.
Don't you fall now —
For I'se still goin', honey,
I'se still climbin',
And life for me ain't been no crystal stair.

The Journey

MARY OLIVER

One day you finally knew
what you had to do, and began,
though the voices around you
kept shouting
their bad advice —
though the whole house
began to tremble

and you felt the old tug
at your ankles.
'Mend my life!'
each voice cried.
But you didn't stop.
You knew what you had to do,
though the wind pried
with its stiff fingers
at the very foundations,
though their melancholy
was terrible.
It was already late
enough, and a wild night,
and the road full of fallen
branches and stones.
But little by little,
as you left their voices behind,
the stars began to burn
through the sheets of clouds,
and there was a new voice
which you slowly
recognised as your own,
that kept you company
as you strode deeper and deeper
into the world,
determined to do
the only thing you could do –
determined to save
the only life you could save.

A Journey

EDWARD FIELD

When he got up that morning everything was different:
He enjoyed the bright spring day
But he did not realise it exactly, he just enjoyed it.

And walking down the street to the railroad station
Past magnolia trees with dying flowers like old socks
It was a long time since he had breathed so simply.

Tears filled his eyes and it felt good
But he held them back
Because men didn't walk around crying in that town.

Waiting on the platform at the station
The fear came over him of something terrible about to happen:
The train was late and he recited the alphabet to keep hold.

And in its time it came screeching in
And as it went on making its usual stops,
People coming and going, telephone poles passing,

He hid his head behind a newspaper
No longer able to hold back the sobs, and willed his eyes
To follow the rational weavings of the seat fabric.

He didn't do anything violent as he had imagined.
He cried for a long time, but when he finally quieted down
A place in him that had been closed like a fist was open,

And at the end of the ride he stood up and got off that train:
And through the streets and in all the places he lived in later on
He walked, himself at last, a man among men,
With such radiance that everyone looked up and wondered.

Musicians in the Underground

DAVID CONSTANTINE

I was descending early, nobody around
And only the usual noises in the corridors which are
The tremor of departures and the wind
When the music started, there was no evading it
Wherever you might have been that morning underground

The wellspring was so deep and all the shafts and stairs
And the winding tiled runs were rinsed
On every level. How well they know
The acoustics of the system. That girl
Who stood in the rush hour at the mouth of one of the chambers

And showed ten thousand people the countenance of an angel
With closed eyes, singing. It was something
Not in our daily speech but still our language
Older, truer. Then how wrong
And slovenly my tongue felt. They visit the body and soul

Of every love and want and the night's lost dreams
They fetch them home. That boy, that faun
Who jumped us slumbering
And rode the lurching car and into the curves and down
The tunnels shivering under our clothes

We had him as conductor, his black horn
Lifted and moaning. These singers,
These couriers through the labyrinth out of the sight of the sun
They are as free as swallows and they know
What the ghosts felt once, and warn us while we can.

The Layers

STANLEY KUNITZ

I have walked through many lives,
some of them my own,
and I am not who I was,
though some principle of being
abides, from which I struggle
not to stray.
When I look behind,
as I am compelled to look
before I can gather strength
to proceed on my journey,
I see the milestones dwindling
toward the horizon
and the slow fires trailing
from the abandoned camp-sites,
over which scavenger angels
wheel on heavy wings.
Oh, I have made myself a tribe
out of my true affections,
and my tribe is scattered!
How shall the heart be reconciled
to its feast of losses?
In a rising wind
the manic dust of my friends,
those who fell along the way,
bitterly stings my face.
Yet I turn, I turn,
exulting somewhat,
with my will intact to go
wherever I need to go,
and every stone on the road
precious to me.

In my darkest night,
when the moon was covered
and I roamed through wreckage,
a nimbus-clouded voice
directed me:
'Live in the layers,
not on the litter.'
Though I lack the art
to decipher it,
no doubt the next chapter
in my book of transformations
is already written.
I am not done with my changes.

Who Makes These Changes?

RUMI

translated from the Persian
by COLEMAN BARKS
with JOHN MOYNE

Who makes these changes?
I shoot an arrow right.
It lands left.
I ride after a deer and find myself
chased by a hog.
I plot to get what I want
and end up in prison.
I dig pits to trap others
and fall in.

I should be suspicious
of what I want.

Autobiography in Five Short Chapters

PORTIA NELSON

I   I walk down the street.
There is a deep hole in the sidewalk
I fall in.
I am lost... I am helpless.
It isn't my fault.
It takes me forever to find a way out.

II   I walk down the same street.
There is a deep hole in the sidewalk.
I pretend I don't see it.
I fall in again.
I can't believe I am in the same place
but, it isn't my fault.
It still takes a long time to get out.

III   I walk down the same street.
There is a deep hole in the sidewalk.
I see it is there.
I still fall in... it's a habit.
My eyes are open
I know where I am.
It is my fault.
I get out immediately.

IV   I walk down the same street.
There is a deep hole in the sidewalk.
I walk around it.

V   I walk down another street.

West Wind [2]

MARY OLIVER

You are young. So you know everything. You leap into the boat and begin rowing. But, listen to me. Without fanfare, without embarrassment, without any doubt, I talk directly to your soul. Listen to me. Lift the oars from the water, let your arms rest, and your heart, and heart's little intelligence, and listen to me. There is life without love. It is not worth a bent penny, or a scuffed shoe. It is not worth the body of a dead dog nine days unburied. When you hear, a mile away and still out of sight, the churn of the water as it begins to swirl and roil, fretting around the sharp rocks – when you hear that unmistakable pounding – when you feel the mist on your mouth and sense ahead the embattlement, the long falls plunging and steaming – then row, row for your life toward it.

Lost

DAVID WAGONER

Stand still. The trees ahead and bushes beside you
Are not lost. Wherever you are is called Here,
And you must treat it as a powerful stranger,
Must ask permission to know it and be known.
The forest breathes. Listen. It answers,
I have made this place around you,
If you leave it, you may come back again, saying Here.
No two trees are the same to Raven.
No two branches are the same to Wren.
If what a tree or a bush does is lost on you,
You are surely lost. Stand still. The forest knows
Where you are. You must let it find you.

Nothing

**CYNTHIA
HUNTINGTON**

These days practicing how to be
without a body. Most often after love
on hot summer nights, when I feel
most alone – not sad, but luminous,
my soul glowing cool as radium – then
when I feel most brave, I start to climb
the night air, like treading water and
think about being nothing substantial,
losing everything but still secured
in this darkfull world. Doing without

all that, beat upon beat, I practice
not hearing my heart, not breathing.
And there are still long grasses,
the tides folding and unfolding, still
the ocean, day and night, and leaves
opening, dinners at a small table with
white candles, fruit and meat.
There is still living and dying and I
have not left you or gone away. I am still
beside you in the dark when you ask
'What are you thinking?' and I tell you:
'Nothing.'

My Body Effervesces

ANNA SWIR

*translated from the Polish
by* CZESŁAW MIŁOSZ
with LEONARD NATHAN

I am born for the second time.
I am light
as the eyelash of the wind.
I froth, I am froth.

I walk dancing,
if I wish, I will soar.
The condensed lightness
of my body
condenses most forcibly
in the lightness of my foot
and its five toes.
The foot skims the earth
which gives way like compressed air.
An elastic duo
of the earth and of the foot. A dance
of liberation.

I am born for the second time,
happiness of the world
came to me again.
My body effervesces,
I think with my body which effervesces.

If I wish
I will soar.

Nothing Is Lost

DANA GIOIA

Nothing is lost. Nothing is so small
that it does not return.
                                    Imagine
that as a child on a day like this
you held a newly minted coin and had
the choice of spending it in any way
you wished.
                        Today the coin comes back to you,
the date rubbed out, the ancient mottoes vague,
the portrait covered with the dull shellac
of anything used up, passed on, disposed of
with something else in view, and always worth
a little less each time.
                                    Now it returns,
and you will think it unimportant, lose
it in your pocket change as one more thing
that's not worth counting, not worth singling out.
That is the mistake you must avoid today.
You sent it on a journey to yourself.
Now hold it in your hand. Accept it as
the little you have earned today.
                                    And realise
that you must choose again but over less.

Sometimes a Man

RAINER MARIA RILKE

translated from the German
by ROBERT BLY

Sometimes a man stands up during supper
and walks outdoors, and keeps on walking,
because of a church that stands somewhere in the East.

And his children say blessings on him as if he were dead.

And another man, who remains inside his own house,
dies there, inside the dishes and in the glasses,
so that his children have to go far out into the world
toward that same church, which he forgot.

Begin

BRENDAN KENNELLY

Begin again to the summoning birds
to the sight of light at the window,
begin to the roar of morning traffic
all along Pembroke Road.
Every beginning is a promise
born in light and dying in dark
determination and exaltation of springtime
flowering the way to work.
Begin to the pageant of queuing girls
the arrogant loneliness of swans in the canal
bridges linking the past and future
old friends passing though with us still.
Begin to the loneliness that cannot end
since it perhaps is what makes us begin,
begin to wonder at unknown faces
at crying birds in the sudden rain
at branches stark in the willing sunlight
at seagulls foraging for bread
at couples sharing a sunny secret
alone together while making good.
Though we live in a world that dreams of ending
that always seems about to give in
something that will not acknowledge conclusion
insists that we forever begin.

My Dead Friends

MARIE HOWE

I have begun,
when I'm weary and can't decide an answer to a bewildering
        question

to ask my dead friends for their opinion
and the answer is often immediate and clear.

Should I take the job? Move to the city? Should I try to conceive
        a child
in my middle age?

They stand in unison shaking their heads and smiling –
        whatever leads
to joy, they always answer,

to more life and less worry. I look into the vase where Billy's
        ashes were –
it's green in there, a green vase,

and I ask Billy if I should return the difficult phone call, and
        he says, yes.
Billy's already gone through the frightening door,

whatever he says I'll do.

Talking to Grief

DENISE LEVERTOV

Ah, grief, I should not treat you
like a homeless dog
who comes to the back door
for a crust, for a meatless bone.
I should trust you.

I should coax you
into the house and give you
your own corner,
a worn mat to lie on
your own water dish.

You think I don't know you've been living
under my porch.
You long for your real place to be readied
before winter comes. You need
your name,
your collar and tag. You need
the right to warn off intruders,
to consider
my house as your own
and me your person
and yourself
my own dog.

Let Evening Come

JANE KENYON

Let the light of late afternoon
shine through chinks in the barn, moving
up the bales as the sun moves down.

Let the cricket take up chafing
as a woman takes up her needles
and her yarn. Let evening come.

Let dew collect on the hoe abandoned
in long grass. Let the stars appear
and the moon disclose her silver horn.

Let the fox go back to its sandy den.
Let the wind die down. Let the shed
go black inside. Let evening come.

To the bottle in the ditch, to the scoop
in the oats, to air in the lung
let evening come.

Let it come, as it will, and don't
be afraid. God does not leave us
comfortless, so let evening come.

When Death Comes

MARY OLIVER

When death comes
like the hungry bear in autumn;
when death comes and takes all the bright coins from his purse

to buy me, and snaps the purse shut;
when death comes
like the measle-pox;

when death comes
like an iceberg between the shoulder blades,

I want to step through the door full of curiosity, wondering:
what is it going to be like, that cottage of darkness?

And therefore I look upon everything
as a brotherhood and a sisterhood,
and I look upon time as no more than an idea,
and I consider eternity as another possibility,

and I think of each life as a flower, as common
as a field daisy, and as singular,

and each name a comfortable music in the mouth,
tending, as all music does, toward silence,

and each body a lion of courage, and something
precious to the earth.

When it's over, I want to say: all my life
I was a bride married to amazement.
I was the bridegroom, taking the world into my arms.

When it's over, I don't want to wonder
if I have made of my life something particular and real.
I don't want to find myself sighing and frightened,
or full of argument.

I don't want to end up simply having visited this world.

4. KNOWING YOURSELF

Ecstatic Longing

J.W. VON **GOETHE**

translated from the German
by DAVID LUKE

Tell it to the wisest only,
For the mob will mock such learning:
I will praise the living creature
That can long for death by burning.

As the candle's quiet gleaming
Cools your nights of hot surrender,
You are touched by strange emotion,
Born again as you engender.

You have passed beyond the shadows:
Snatched aloft, you shall discover
New desire and higher union:
Thrall of darkness now is over.

Distance tires you not nor hinders,
On you come with fated flight
Till, poor moth, at last you perish
In the flame, in love with light.

Die into becoming! Grasp
This, or sad and weary
Shall your sojourn ever be
On the dark earth dreary.

THREE POEMS FROM

The World

CZESŁAW MIŁOSZ

translated from the Polish
by CZESLAW MILOSZ

Faith

Faith is in you whenever you look
At a dewdrop or a floating leaf
And know that they are because they have to be.
Even if you close your eyes and dream up things
The world will remain as it has always been
And the leaf will be carried by the waters of the river.

You have faith also when you hurt your foot
Against a sharp rock and you know
That rocks are here to hurt our feet.
See the long shadow that is cast by the tree?
We and the flowers throw shadows on the earth.
What has no shadow has no strength to live.

Hope

Hope is with you when you believe
The earth is not a dream but living flesh,
That sight, touch, and hearing do not lie,
That all things you have ever seen here
Are like a garden looked at from a gate.

You cannot enter. But you're sure it's there.
Could we but look more clearly and wisely
We might discover somewhere in the garden
A strange new flower and an unnamed star.

Some people say we should not trust our eyes,
That there is nothing, just a seeming,
These are the ones who have no hope.
They think that the moment we turn away,
The world, behind our backs, ceases to exist,
As if snatched up by the hands of thieves.

Love

Love means to learn to look at yourself
The way one looks at distant things
For you are only one thing among many.
And whoever sees that way heals his heart,
Without knowing it, from various ills –
A bird and a tree say to him: Friend.

Then he wants to use himself and things
So that they stand in the glow of ripeness.
It doesn't matter whether he knows what he serves:
Who serves best doesn't always understand.

Happiness

JANE KENYON

There's just no accounting for happiness,
or the way it turns up like a prodigal
who comes back to the dust at your feet
having squandered a fortune far away.

And how can you not forgive?
You make a feast in honor of what
was lost, and take from its place the finest
garment, which you saved for an occasion
you could not imagine, and you weep night and day
to know that you were not abandoned,
that happiness saved its most extreme form
for you alone.

No, happiness is the uncle you never
knew about, who flies a single-engine plane
onto the grassy landing strip, hitchhikes
into town, and inquires at every door
until he finds you asleep midafternoon
as you so often are during the unmerciful
hours of your despair.

It comes to the monk in his cell.
It comes to the woman sweeping the street
with a birch broom, to the child
whose mother has passed out from drink.
It comes to the lover, to the dog chewing
a sock, to the pusher, to the basket maker,
and to the clerk stacking cans of carrots
in the night.

It even comes to the boulder
in the perpetual shade of pine barrens,
to rain falling on the open sea,
to the wineglass, weary of holding wine.

Kindness

**NAOMI
SHIHAB NYE**

[*Colombia*]

Before you know what kindness really is
you must lose things,
feel the future dissolve in a moment
like salt in a weakened broth.
What you held in your hand,
what you counted and carefully saved,
all this must go so you know
how desolate the landscape can be
between the regions of kindness.
How you ride and ride
thinking the bus will never stop,
the passengers eating maize and chicken
will stare out the window forever.

Before you learn the tender gravity of kindness,
you must travel where the Indian in a white poncho
lies dead by the side of the road.
You must see how this could be you,
how he too was someone
who journeyed through the night with plans
and the simple breath that kept him alive.

Before you know kindness as the deepest thing inside,
you must know sorrow as the other deepest thing.
You must wake up with sorrow.
You must speak to it till your voice
catches the thread of all sorrows
and you see the size of the cloth.

Then it is only kindness that makes sense anymore,
only kindness that ties your shoes
and sends you out into the day to mail letters and purchase bread,
only kindness that raises its head
from the crowd of the world to say
It is I you have been looking for,
and then goes with you everywhere
like a shadow or a friend.

Song for Nobody

THOMAS MERTON

A yellow flower
(Light and spirit)
Sings by itself
For nobody.

A golden spirit
(Light and emptiness)
Sings without a word
By itself.

Let no one touch this gentle sun
In whose dark eye
Someone is awake.

(No light, no gold, no name, no color
And no thought:
O, wide awake!)

A golden heaven
Sings by itself
A song to nobody.

Speak You Too

PAUL CELAN

translated from the German
by JOHN FELSTINER

Speak you too,
speak as the last,
say out your say.

Speak –
But don't split off No from Yes.
Give your say this meaning too:
give it the shadow.

Give it shadow enough,
give it as much
as you see spread round you from
midnight to midday and midnight.

Look around:
see how things all come alive –
By death! Alive!
Speaks true who speaks shadow.

But now the place shrinks, where you stand:
Where now, shadow-stripped, where?
Climb. Grope upwards.
Thinner you grow, less knowable, finer!
Finer: a thread
the star wants to descend on:
so as to swim down below, down here
where it sees itself shimmer: in the swell
of wandering words.

A Zero-Circle

RUMI

translated from the Persian
by JOHN MOYNE
& COLEMAN BARKS

Be helpless, dumbfounded,
unable to say yes or no.

Then a stretcher will come
from grace to gather us up.

We are too dull-eyed to see the beauty.
If we say *Yes we can*, we'll be lying.

If we say *No, we don't see it,*
that *No* will behead us
and shut tight our window into spirit.

So let us rather not be sure of anything,
beside ourselves, and only that, so
miraculous beings come running to help.

Crazed, lying in a zero-circle, mute,
we will be saying finally,
with tremendous eloquence, *Lead us.*

When we've totally surrendered to that beauty,
we'll become a mighty kindness.

'After great pain, a formal feeling comes...'

EMILY DICKINSON

After great pain, a formal feeling comes –
The Nerves sit ceremonious, like Tombs –
The stiff Heart questions 'was it He, that bore',
And 'Yesterday, or Centuries before'?

The Feet, mechanical, go round –
A Wooden way
Of Ground, or Air, or Ought –
Regardless grown,
A Quartz contentment, like a stone –

This is the Hour of Lead –
Remembered, if outlived,
As Freezing persons, recollect the Snow –
First – Chill – then Stupor – then the letting go –

Four A.M.

**WISŁAWA
SZYMBORSKA**

translated from the Polish
by STANISLAW BARANCZAK
and CLARE CAVANAGH

The hour between night and day.
The hour between toss and turn.
The hour of thirty-year-olds.

The hour swept clean for roosters' crowing.
The hour when the earth takes back its warm embrace.
The hour of cool drafts from extinguished stars.
The hour of do-we-vanish-too-without-a-trace.

Empty hour.
Hollow. Vain.
Rock bottom of all the other hours.

No one feels fine at four A.M.
If ants feel fine at four A.M.,
we're happy for the ants. And let five A.M. come
if we've got to go on living.

Things

FLEUR ADCOCK

There are worse things than having behaved foolishly in public.
There are worse things than these miniature betrayals,
committed or endured or suspected; there are worse things
than not being able to sleep for thinking about them.
It is 5 A.M. All the worse things come stalking in
and stand icily about the bed looking worse and worse and worse.

I Sit in My Room

JEAN TOOMER

I sit in my room.
The thick adobe walls
Are transparent to mountains,
The mountains move in;
I sit among mountains.

I, who am no more,
Having lost myself to let the world in,
This world of black and bronze mesas
Canyoned by rivers from the higher hills.
I am the hills,
I am the mountains and the dark trees thereon;
I am the storm,
I am this day and all revealed,
Blue without boundary,
Bright without limit
Selfless at this entrance to the universe.

Anger

CÉSAR VALLEJO

translated from the Spanish
by THOMAS MERTON

[26 October 1937/1939]

Anger which breaks a man into children,
Which breaks the child into two equal birds,
And after that the bird into a pair of little eggs:
The poor man's anger
Has one oil against two vinegars.

Anger which breaks a tree into leaves
And the leaf into unequal buds
And the bud into telescopic grooves;
The poor man's anger
Has two rivers against many seas.

Anger which breaks good into doubts
And doubt into three similar arcs
And then the arc into unexpected tombs;
The poor man's anger
Has one steel against two daggers.

Anger which breaks the soul into bodies
And the body into dissimilar organs
And the organ into octave thoughts;
The poor man's anger
Has one central fire against two craters.

Hope

EDITH SÖDERGRAN

translated from the Finland Swedish
by DAVID McDUFF

[September 1918]

I want to be unconstrained –
therefore I care not a fig for noble styles.
I roll up my sleeves.
The poem's dough is rising...
Oh what a pity
that I cannot bake cathedrals...
Highness of forms –
goal of persistent longing.
Child of the present –
does your spirit not have a proper shell?
Before I die
I shall bake a cathedral.

Strong in the Rain

**KENJI
MIYAZAWA**

*translated from the Japanese
by* ROGER PULVERS

[3 November 1931]

Strong in the rain
Strong in the wind
Strong against the summer heat and snow
He is healthy and robust
Free from desire
He never loses his temper
Nor the quiet smile on his lips
He eats four *go* of unpolished rice
Miso and a few vegetables a day
He does not consider himself
In whatever occurs...his understanding
Comes from observation and experience
And he never loses sight of things
He lives in a little thatched-roof hut
In a field in the shadows of a pine tree grove
If there is a sick child in the east
He goes there to nurse the child
If there's a tired mother in the west
He goes to her and carries her sheaves
If someone is near death in the south
He goes and says, 'Don't be afraid'
If there are strife and lawsuits in the north
He demands that the people put an end to their pettiness
He weeps at the time of drought
He plods about at a loss during the cold summer
Everyone calls him Blockhead
No one sings his praises
Or takes him to heart...

That is the kind of person
I want to be

Me

CHAIRIL ANWAR

translated from the Indonesian
by BURTON RAFFEL

When my time comes
No one's going to cry for me,
And you won't, either

The hell with all those tears!

I'm a wild beast
Driven out of the herd

Bullets may pierce my skin
But I'll keep coming,

Carrying forward my wounds and my pain
Attacking
Attacking
Until suffering disappears

And I won't give a damn

I want to live another thousand years

Triumph
of being...

EDITH SÖDERGRAN

translated from
the Finland Swedish
by DAVID McDUFF

[1916]

What have I to fear? I am a part of infinity,
I am a part of the all's great power,
a lonely world inside millions of worlds,
like a star of the first degree that fades last.
Triumph of living, triumph of breathing, triumph of being!
Triumph of feeling time run ice-cold through one's veins
and of hearing the silent river of the night
and of standing on the mountain under the sun.
I walk on sun, I stand on sun,
I know of nothing else than sun.

Time – convertress, time – destructress, time – enchantress,
do you come with new schemes, a thousand tricks to offer
  me existence
as a little seed, as a coiled snake, as a rock amidst the sea?
Time – you murderess – leave me!
The sun fills my breast with sweet honey up to the brim
and she says: all stars fade at last, but they always shine
  without fear.

Love after Love

DEREK WALCOTT

The time will come
when, with elation,
you will greet yourself arriving
at your own door, in your own mirror
and each will smile at the other's welcome,

and say, sit here. Eat.
You will love again the stranger who was your self.
Give wine. Give bread, Give back your heart
to itself, to the stranger who has loved you

all your life, whom you ignored
for another, who knows you by heart.
Take down the love letters from the bookshelf,

the photographs, the desperate notes,
peel your own image from the mirror.
Sit. Feast on your life.

Mandorla

PAUL CELAN

translated from the German
by JOHN FELSTINER

In the almond – what stands in the almond?
The Nothing.
In the almond stands Nothing.
There it stands and stands.

In the Nothing – who stands there? The King.
There stands the King, the King.
There he stands and stands.

      Jewish curls, no gray for you.

And your eye – whereto stands your eye?
Your eye stands opposite the almond.
Your eye, the Nothing it stands opposite.
It stands by the King.
So it stands and stands.

      Human curls, no gray for you.
      Empty almond, kingly blue.

Still I Rise

MAYA ANGELOU

You may write me down in history
With your bitter, twisted lies,
You may trod me in the very dirt
But still, like dust, I'll rise.

Does my sassiness upset you?
Why are you beset with gloom?
'Cause I walk like I've got oil wells
Pumping in my living room.

Just like moons and like suns,
With the certainty of tides,
Just like hopes springing high,
Still I'll rise.

Did you want to see me broken?
Bowed head and lowered eyes?
Shoulders falling down like teardrops,
Weakened by my soulful cries?

Does my haughtiness offend you?
Don't you take it awful hard
'Cause I laugh like I've got gold mines
Diggin' in my own backyard.

You may shoot me with your words,
You may cut me with your eyes,
You may kill me with your hatefulness,
But still, like air, I'll rise.

Does my sexiness upset you?
Does it come as a surprise
That I dance like I've got diamonds
At the meeting of my thighs?

Out of the huts of history's shame
I rise
Up from a past that's rooted in pain
I rise
I'm a black ocean, leaping and wide,
Welling and swelling I bear in the tide.

Leaving behind nights of terror and fear
I rise
Into a daybreak that's wondrously clear
I rise
Bringing the gifts that my ancestors gave,
I am the dream and the hope of the slave.
I rise
I rise
I rise.

5. BELIEVING BODY AND SOUL

The Third Body

ROBERT BLY

A man and a woman sit near each other, and they do not long
At this moment to be older, or younger, or born
In any other nation, or any other time, or any other place.
They are content to be where they are, talking or not talking.
Their breaths together feed someone whom we do not know.
The man sees the way his fingers move;
He sees her hands close around a book she hands to him.
They obey a third body that they share in common.
They have promised to love that body.
Age may come; parting may come; death will come!
A man and a woman sit near each other;
As they breathe they feed someone we do not know,
Someone we know of, whom we have never seen.

Mirages

KAPKA KASSABOVA

Waking up in the same skin isn't enough.
You need more and more evidence
of who it is that
wakes up in the same skin.

But what evidence?
Reality is unreliable: a whirlwind
of dust that appears
and disappears every day.

Your thirst stretches out its white dunes.

Every day in the dust
you distinguish

not islands but their darkness
heaped on the polished mirror of a sea.

Not doors but their shadows
slammed in the house of wind.

Not lighthouses but their half-second SOS
in red, green and yellow.

Not language but languages.

Not your hand closing a curtain
but a hand.

And the day is over,
not wiser than the night in which
you waited for something
that came and wasn't what you'd waited for.

My real dwelling

IKKYU

translated from the Japanese
by JOHN STEVENS

My real dwelling
Has no pillars
And no roof either
So rain cannot soak it
And wind cannot blow it down!

A Riddle:
Of the Soul

M.K. JOSEPH

I cannot give
   Unless I have
I cannot have
   Unless I save
Unless I have
   I cannot save
Unless I give
   I cannot have.

Unless I live
   I cannot be
Unless I am
   I cannot seem
I cannot be
   Unless I seem
I cannot live
   Unless I am.

I cannot be
   Unless I give
I cannot have
   Unless I die
Unless I grieve
   I cannot love
Unless I die
   I cannot live.

A Few Words on the Soul

WISŁAWA SZYMBORSKA

translated from the Polish
by STANISLAW BARANCZAK
& CLARE CAVANAGH

We have a soul at times.
No one's got it nonstop,
for keeps.

Day after day,
year after year
may pass without it.

Sometimes
it will settle for a while
only in childhood's fears and raptures.
Sometimes only in astonishment
that we are old.

It rarely lends a hand
in uphill tasks,
like moving furniture,
or lifting luggage,
or going miles in shoes that pinch.

It usually steps out
whenever meat needs chopping
or forms have to be filled.

For every thousand conversations
it participates in one,
if even that,
since it prefers silence.

Just when our body goes from ache to pain,
it slips off duty.

It's picky:
it doesn't like seeing us in crowds,
our hustling for a dubious advantage
and creaky machinations make it sick.

Joy and sorrow
aren't two different feelings for it.
It attends us
only when the two are joined.

We can count on it
when we're sure of nothing
and curious about everything.

Among the material objects
it favors clocks with pendulums
and mirrors, which keep on working
even when no one is looking.

It won't say where it comes from
or when it's taking off again,
though it's clearly expecting such questions.

We need it
but apparently
it needs us
for some reason too.

Some Questions You Might Ask

MARY OLIVER

Is the soul solid, like iron?
Or is it tender and breakable, like
the wings of a moth in the beak of the owl?
Who has it, and who doesn't?
I keep looking around me.
The face of the moose is as sad
as the face of Jesus.
The swan opens her white wings slowly.
In the fall, the black bear carries leaves into the darkness.
One question leads to another.
Does it have a shape? Like an iceberg?
Like the eye of a hummingbird?
Does it have one lung, like the snake and the scallop?
Why should I have it, and not the anteater
who loves her children?
Why should I have it, and not the camel?
Come to think of it, what about the maple trees?
What about the blue iris?
What about all the little stones, sitting alone in the moonlight?
What about roses, and lemons, and their shining leaves?
What about the grass?

How to
Regain
Your Soul

**WILLIAM
STAFFORD**

Come down Canyon Creek on a summer afternoon
that one place where the valley floor opens out. You will see
the white butterflies. Because of the way shadows
come off those vertical rocks in the west, there are
shafts of sunlight hitting the river and a deep
long purple gorge straight ahead. Put down your pack.

Above, air sighs in the pines. It was this way
when Rome was clanging, when Troy was being built,
when campfires lighted caves. The white butterflies dance
by the thousands in the still sunshine. Suddenly, anything
could happen to you. Your soul pulls toward the canyon
and then shines back through the white wings to be you again.

Haiku

SHIKI

White butterfly
darting among pinks –
whose spirit?

translated from the Japanese
by LUCIEN STRYK
& TAKAHASHI IKEMOTO

Concerning the Atoms of the Soul

JOHN GLENDAY

Someone explained once how the pieces of what we are
fall downwards at the same rate
as the Universe.
The atoms of us, falling towards the centre

of whatever everything is. And we don't see it.
We only sense their slight drag in the lifting hand.
That's what weight is, that communal process of falling.
Furthermore, those atoms carry hooks, like burrs,

hooks catching like hooks, like clinging to like,
that's what keeps us from becoming something else,
and why in early love, we sometimes
feel the tug of the heart snagging on another's heart.

Only the atoms of the soul are perfect spheres
with no means of holding on to the world
or perhaps no need for holding on,
and so they fall through our lives catching

against nothing, like perfect rain,
and in the end, he wrote, mix in that common well of light
at the centre of whatever the suspected
centre is, or might have been.

Unmarked Boxes

RUMI

translated from the Persian
by COLEMAN BARKS
with JOHN MOYNE

Don't grieve. Anything you lose comes round
in another form. The child weaned from mother's milk
now drinks wine and honey mixed.

God's joy moves from unmarked box to unmarked box,
from cell to cell. As rainwater, down into flowerbed.
As roses, up from ground.
Now it looks like a plate of rice and fish,
now a cliff covered with vines,
now a horse being saddled.
It hides within these,
till one day it cracks them open.

Part of the self leaves the body when we sleep
and changes shape. You might say, 'Last night
I was a cypress tree, a small bed of tulips,
a field of grapevines.' Then the phantasm goes away.
You're back in the room.
I don't want to make anyone fearful.
Hear what's behind what I say.

Tatatumtum, tatum, tatadum.
There's the light gold of wheat in the sun
and the gold of bread made from that wheat.
I have neither. I'm only talking about them,

as a town in the desert looks up
at stars on a clear night.

The Ringing Chamber

PAULINE STAINER

I was four months gone –
my breasts already tender
against the bell-ropes;

we were ringing quarter-peals,
the sun flooding the bell-chamber,
the dust rippling between the joists

when the child quickened,
fluttered against the changes;
and suddenly through the clerestory

I saw that colder quickening –
random, reciprocal –
cloudshadow

and the flaxfield
like water under the wind.

Horse

CHASE TWICHELL

I've never seen a soul detached from its gender,
but I'd like to. I'd like to see my own that way,
free of its female tethers. Maybe it would be like
riding a horse. The rider's the human one,
but everyone looks at the horse.

A Place to Sit

KABIR

translated from the Hindi
by ROBERT BLY

Don't go outside your house to see flowers.
My friend, don't bother with that excursion.
Inside your body there are flowers.
One flower has a thousand petals.
That will do for a place to sit.
Sitting there you will have a glimpse of beauty
inside the body and out of it,
before gardens and after gardens.

Everything You See

RUMI

translated from the Persian
by ANDREW HARVEY

Everything you see has its roots in the unseen world.
     The forms may change, yet the essence remains the same.
Every wonderful sight will vanish, every sweet word will fade,
     But do not be disheartened,
The source they come from is eternal, growing,
     Branching out, giving new life and new joy.
Why do you weep?
     The source is within you
And this whole world is springing up from it.

The Swing

KABIR

translated from the Hindi
by ROBERT BLY

Between the conscious and the unconscious, the mind has put
          up a swing:
all earth creatures, even the supernovas, sway between these
          two trees,
and it never winds down.

Angels, animals, humans, insects by the million, also the
          wheeling sun and moon;
ages go by, and it goes on.

Everything is swinging: heaven, earth, water, fire,
and the secret one slowly growing a body.
Kabir saw that for fifteen seconds, and it made him a servant
          for life.

6. WHAT PRAYER?

Prayer

IMTIAZ DHARKER

The place is full of worshippers.
You can tell by the sandals
piled outside, the owners' prints
worn into leather, rubber, plastic,
a picture clearer than their faces
put together, with some originality,
brows and eyes, the slant
of cheek to chin.

What prayer are they whispering?
Each one has left a mark,
the perfect pattern of a need,
sole and heel and toe
in dark curved patches,
heels worn down,
thongs ragged, mended many times.
So many shuffling hopes,
pounded into print,
as clear as the pages of holy books,
illuminated with the glint
of gold around the lettering.

What are they whispering?
Outside, in the sun,
such a quiet crowd
of shoes, thrown together
like a thousand prayers
washing against the walls of God.

Prayer

CAROL ANN DUFFY

Some days, although we cannot pray, a prayer
utters itself. So, a woman will lift
her head from the sieve of her hands and stare
at the minims sung by a tree, a sudden gift.

Some nights, although we are faithless, the truth
enters our hearts, that small familiar pain;
then a man will stand stock-still, hearing his youth
in the distant Latin chanting of a train.

Pray for us now. Grade I piano scales
console the lodger looking out across
a Midlands town. Then dusk, and someone calls
a child's name as though they named their loss.

Darkness outside. Inside, the radio's prayer –
Rockall. Malin. Dogger. Finisterre.

What you need to know for praying

GILLIAN ALLNUTT

You need to know that no one has been here before,
not even you, though you are as ever

kneeling on the oblong Indian rug, its faded
tree, its dry blue birds.

You may imagine that
they sing. You need to know that

everyone who was or is or will be's
here with you in your always

unswept room. You may imagine it's an ark, the first or last,
and that the earth spins, scattering dust.

You need to know your heart
will beat

its wings,
will not berate you for imagining

you've sent it out,
a solitary raven, on its way from Ararat.

Trying to Pray

JAMES WRIGHT

This time, I have left my body behind me, crying
In its dark thorns.
Still,
There are good things in this world.
It is dusk.
It is the good darkness
Of women's hands that touch loaves.
The spirit of a tree begins to move.
I touch leaves.
I close my eyes, and think of water.

Prayer

GALWAY KINNELL

Whatever happens. Whatever
what is is is what
I want. Only that. But that.

Eagle Poem

JOY HARJO

To pray you open your whole self
To sky, to earth, to sun, to moon
To one whole voice that is you.
And know there is more
That you can't see, can't hear,
Can't know except in moments
Steadily growing, and in languages
That aren't always sound but other
Circles of motion.
Like eagle that Sunday morning
Over Salt River. Circled in blue sky
In wind, swept our hearts clean
With sacred wings.
We see you, see ourselves and know
That we must take the utmost care
And kindness in all things.
Breathe in, knowing we are made of
All this, and breathe, knowing
We are truly blessed because we
Were born, and die soon within a
True circle of motion,
Like eagle rounding out the morning
Inside us.
We pray that it will be done
In beauty.
In beauty.

Prayer

**CAROLYN
FORCHÉ**

Begin again among the poorest, moments off, in another time
and place.
Belongings gathered in the last hour, visible invisible:
Tin spoon, teacup, tremble of tray, carpet hanging from sorrow's
balcony.
Say goodbye to everything. With a wave of your hand, gesture
to all you have known.
Begin with bread torn from bread, beans given to the hungriest,
a carcass of flies.
Take the polished stillness from a locked church, prayer notes
left between stones.
Answer them and hoist in your net voices from the troubled
hours.
Sleep only when the least among them sleeps, and then only
until the birds.
Make the flatbed truck your time and place. Make the least daily
wage your value.
Language will rise then like language from the mouth of a still
river. No one's mouth.
Bring night to your imaginings. Bring the darkest passage of
your holy book.

7.   TALKING TO GOD

FROM

*Eleven
Addresses
to the Lord* [1]

JOHN BERRYMAN

Master of beauty, craftsman of the snowflake,
inimitable contriver,
endower of Earth so gorgeous & different from the boring Moon,
thank you for such as it is my gift.

I have made up a morning prayer to you
containing with precision everything that most matters.
'According to Thy will' the thing begins.
It took me off & on two days. It does not aim at eloquence.

You have come to my rescue again & again
in my impassable, sometimes despairing years.
You have allowed my brilliant friends to destroy themselves
and I am still here, severely damaged, but functioning.

Unknowable, as I am unknown to my guinea pigs:
how can I "love" you?
I only as far as gratitude & awe
confidently & absolutely go.

I have no idea whether we live again.
It doesn't seem likely
from either the scientific or the philosophical point of view
but certainly all things are possible to you,

and I believe as fixedly in the Resurrection-appearances to
      Peter and to Paul
as I believe I sit in this blue chair.
Only that may have been a special case
to establish their initiatory faith.

Whatever your end may be, accept my amazement.
May I stand until death forever at attention
for any your least instruction or enlightenment.
I even feel sure you will assist me again, Master of insight &
      beauty.

The Priest in the Pulpit

DAVID SCOTT

Will it last, this opening of the heart
to the Word, or will the new ways,
the film, the television, the e-mail,
dislodge us from the art of oratory?
Climbing the steps, taking off the paper clip,
remembering not to put it in my mouth,
the text, the Greek, the joke, the text again,
all this, O God, you know, as well as asking you
to make all things, especially the haste,
respectable. As the spiral notebooks rust
along the shelves, who knows how a word
in the thickest of the sermon's stickiest part,
might just have winged its way into the heart
of one young stranger there, and taken roost.

Demiurge

D.H. LAWRENCE

They say that reality exists only in the spirit
that corporal existence is a kind of death
that pure being is bodiless
that the idea of the form precedes the form substantial.

But what nonsense it is!
as if any Mind could have imagined a lobster
dozing in the under-deeps, then reaching out a savage and iron claw!

Even the mind of God can only imagine
those things that have become themselves:
bodies and presences, here and now, creatures with a foothold in
        creation
even if it is only a lobster on tiptoe.

Religion knows better than philosophy.
Religion knows that Jesus was never Jesus
till he was born from a womb, and ate soup and bread
and grew up, and became, in the wonder of creation, Jesus,
with a body and with needs, and a lovely spirit.

Let me tell you about my marvelous god

SUSAN STEWART

Let me tell you about my marvelous god, how he hides in
      the hexagons
of the bees, how the drought that wrings its leather hands
above the world is of his making, as well as the rain in the
      quiet minutes
that leave only thoughts of rain.
An atom is working and working, an atom is working in deepest
night, then bursting like the farthest star; it is far
smaller than a pinprick, far smaller than a zero and it has no
will, no will toward us.
This is why the heart has paced and paced,
will pace and pace across the field where yarrow
was and now is dust. A leaf catches
in a bone. The burrow's shut by a tumbled clod
and the roots, upturned, are hot to the touch.
How my god is a feathered and whirling thing; you will singe
      your arm
when you pluck him from the air,
when you pluck him from that sky
where grieving swirls, and you will burn again
throwing him back.

God Says
Yes To Me

KAYLIN HAUGHT

I asked God if it was okay to be melodramatic
and she said yes
I asked her if it was okay to be short
and she said it sure is
I asked her if I could wear nail polish
or not wear nail polish
and she said honey
she calls me that sometimes
she said you can do just exactly
what you want to
Thanks God I said
And is it even okay if I don't paragraph
my letters
Sweetcakes God said
who knows where she picked that up
what I'm telling you is
Yes Yes Yes

Sheep Fair Day

KERRY HARDIE

The real aim is not to see God in all things, it is that God, through us, should see the things that we see.
SIMONE WEIL

I took God with me to the sheep fair. I said, 'Look
there's Liv, sitting on the wall, waiting;
these are pens, these are sheep,
this is their shit we are walking in, this is their fear.
See that man over there, stepping along the low walls
between pens, eyes always watching,
mouth always talking, he is the auctioneer.
That is wind in the ash trees above, that is sun
splashing us with running light and dark.
Those men over there, the ones with their faces sealed,
are buying or selling. Beyond in the ring
where the beasts pour in, huddle and rush,
the hoggets are auctioned in lots.
And that woman with the ruddy face and the home-cut hair
and a new child on her arm, that is how it is to be woman
with the milk running, sitting on wooden boards
in this shit-milky place of animals and birth and death
as the bidding rises and falls.'

Then I went back outside and found Fintan.
I showed God his hand as he sat on the rails,
how he let it trail down and his fingers played
in the curly back of a ewe. Fintan's a sheep-man
he's deep into sheep, though it's cattle he keeps now,
for sound commercial reasons.
                              'Feel that,' I said,
'feel with my heart the force in that hand
that's twining her wool as he talks.'

Then I went with Fintan and Liv to Refreshments,
I let God sip tea, boiling hot, from a cup,
and I lent God my fingers to feel how they burned
when I tripped on a stone and it slopped.
'This is hurt,' I said, 'there'll be more.'
And the morning wore on and the sun climbed
and God felt how it is when I stand too long,
how the sickness rises, how the muscles burn.

Later, at the back end of the afternoon,
I went down to swim in the green slide of river,
I worked my way under the bridge, against the current,
then I showed how it is to turn onto your back
with, above you and a long way up, two gossiping pigeons,
and a clump of valerian, holding itself to the sky.
I remarked on the stone arch as I drifted through it,
how it dapples with sunlight from the water,
how the bridge hunkers down, crouching low in its track
and roars when a lorry drives over.

And later again, in the kitchen,
wrung out, at day's ending, and empty,
I showed how it feels
to undo yourself,
to dissolve, and grow age-old, nameless:

woman sweeping a floor, darkness growing.

Summers and Springs

JAAN KAPLINSKI

translated from
the Estonian
by JAAN KAPLINSKI
with FIONA SAMPSON

God has left us: I felt this clearly
loosening the earth around a rhubarb plant.
It was black and moist. I don't know where he is,
only a shelf full of sacred books remains of him,
a couple of wax candles, a prayer wheel and a little bell.
Coming back to the house I thought
there might still be something: the smell of lilac and honeysuckle.
Then suddenly I imagined a child's face
there, on the other side, in eternity
looking here, into time, regarding wide-eyed
our comings, goings and doings in this time-aquarium
under the light of the sun going down;
and falling asleep under a water-lily leaf
somewhere far away in the west.

Missing God

DENNIS O'DRISCOLL

His grace is no longer called for
before meals: farmed fish multiply
without His intercession.
Bread production rises through
disease-resistant grains devised
scientifically to mitigate His faults.

Yet, though we rebelled against Him
like adolescents, uplifted to see
an oppressive father banished –
a bearded hermit – to the desert,
we confess to missing Him at times.

Miss Him during the civil wedding
when, at the blossomy altar
of the registrar's desk, we wait in vain
to be fed a line containing words
like 'everlasting' and 'divine'.

Miss Him when the TV scientist
explains the cosmos through equations,
leaving our planet to revolve on its axis
aimlessly, a wheel skidding in snow.

Miss Him when the radio catches a snatch
of plainchant from some echoey priory;
when the gospel choir raises its collective voice
to ask *Shall We Gather at the River?*
or the forces of the oratorio converge
on *I Know That My Redeemer Liveth*
and our contracted hearts lose a beat.

Miss Him when a choked voice at
the crematorium recites the poem
about fearing no more the heat of the sun.

Miss Him when we stand in judgement
on a lank Crucifixion in an art museum,
its stripe-like ribs testifying to rank.

Miss Him when the gamma-rays
recorded on the satellite graph
seem arranged into a celestial score,
the music of the spheres,
the *Ave Verum Corpus* of the observatory lab.

Miss Him when we stumble on the breast lump
for the first time and an involuntary prayer
escapes our lips; when a shadow crosses
our bodies on an x-ray screen; when we receive
a transfusion of foaming blood
sacrificed anonymously to save life.

Miss Him when we exclaim His name
spontaneously in awe or anger
as a woman in the birth ward
calls to her long-dead mother.

Miss Him when the linen-covered
dining-table holds warm bread rolls,
shiny glasses of red wine.

Miss Him when a dove swoops
from the orange grove in a tourist village
just as the monastery bell begins to take its toll.

Miss Him when our journey leads us
under leaves of Gothic tracery, an arch
of overlapping branches that meet
like hands in Michelangelo's *Creation*.

Miss Him when, trudging past a church,
we catch a residual blast of incense,
a perfume on par with the fresh-baked loaf
which Milosz compared to happiness.

Miss Him when our newly-fitted kitchen
comes in Shaker-style and we order
a matching set of Mother Ann Lee chairs.

Miss Him when we listen to the prophecy
of astronomers that the visible galaxies
will recede as the universe expands.

Miss Him when the sunset makes
its presence felt in the stained glass
window of the fake antique lounge bar.

Miss Him the way an uncoupled glider
riding the evening thermals misses its tug.

Miss Him, as the lovers shrugging
shoulders outside the cheap hotel
ponder what their next move should be.

Even feel nostalgic, odd days,
for His Second Coming,
like standing in the brick
dome of a dovecote
after the birds have flown.

The Other World

ANNA KAMIENSKA

translated from the Polish
by TOMAS P. KRZESZOWSKI
& DESMOND GRAHAM

I don't believe in the other world

But also I don't believe in this world
unless it is pierced by light

I believe in the body of a woman
hit by a car in the street

I believe in bodies
stopped in a hurry
in a gesture in mid-pursuit
as something long expected
was about to happen
as if in an instant
sense was to lift up
its finger

I believe in a blind eye
in a deaf ear
in a lame foot
in a crease at the temple
in red fire on the cheek

I believe in bodies lying
in the trust of sleep
in the patience of old age
in the weakness of the unborn

I believe in a hair from the dead
left on a brown beret

I believe that brilliance
is multiplied miraculously
onto all things

Even the May bug
which fumbles about on its back
helpless as a little puppy

I believe that the rain
stitches sky to earth
and with the rain the angels
visibly descend
like winged frogs

I don't believe in this world
empty
like a railway station before dawn
when all the trains have gone
to the other world

The world is one
especially when it wakes up in dew
and the Lord walks about
among the bushes
of animal and human dreams

Credo

FIONA FARRELL

I believe in
the gingerbread man.
Who wouldn't run,
given the circumstances?

But not the Father,
not the Son.

I believe in
forgiveness.

But not in sin.

I believe in
communion:
bread wine
apples and us all
happy at table.

But not in saints.

I believe in
life. You have to,
don't you, being alive?

But not everlasting.

Those immortelles, petals
fallen like yellow teeth
in the tomb, bearing the
form of flowers.

But not the scent,
not the breath.

Why I Am Not a Buddhist

MOLLY PEACOCK

I love desire, the state of want and thought
of how to get; building a kingdom in a soul
requires desire. I love the things I've sought –
you in your beltless bathrobe, tongues of cash that loll
from my billfold – and love what I want: clothes,
houses, redemption. Can a new mauve suit
equal God? Oh no, desire is ranked. To lose
a loved pen is not like losing faith. Acute
desire for nut gateau is driven out by death,
but the cake on its plate has meaning,
even when love is endangered and nothing matters.
For my mother, health; for my sister, bereft,
wholeness. But why is desire suffering?
Because want leaves a world in tatters?
How else but in tatters should a world be?
A columned porch set high above a lake.
Here, take my money. A loved face in agony,
the spirit gone. Here, use my rags of love.

Meta-A
and the A
of Absolutes

JAY WRIGHT

I write my God in blue.
I run my gods upstream on flimsy rafts.
I bathe my goddesses in foam, in moonlight.
I take my reasons from my mother's snuff breath,
or from an old woman, sitting with a lemonade,
at twilight, on the desert's steps.
Brown by day and black by night,
my God has wings that open to no reason.
He scutters from the touch of old men's eyes,
scutters from the smell of wisdom, an orb
of light leaping from a fire.
Press him he bleeds.
When you take your hand to sacred water,
there is no sign of any wound.
And so I call him supreme, great artist,
judge of time, scholar of all living event,
the possible prophet of the possible event.
Blind men, on bourbon, with guitars,
blind men with their scars dulled by kola,
blind men seeking the shelter of a raindrop,
blind men in corn, blind men in steel,
reason by their lights that our tongues
are free, our tongues will redeem us.
Speech is the fact, and the fact is true.
What is moves, and what is moving is.
We cling to these contradictions.
We know we will become our contradictions,
our complex body's-own desire.
Yet speech is not the limit of our vision.
The ear entices itself with any sound.

The skin will caress whatever tone
or temperament that rises or descends.
The bones will set themselves to a dance.
The blood will argue with a bird in flight.
The heart will scale the dew from an old chalice,
brush and thrill to an old bone.
And yet there is no sign to arrest us
                              from the possible.
We remain at rest there, in transit
from our knowing to our knowledge.
So I would set a limit where I meet my logic.
I would clamber from my own cave
into the curve of sign, an alphabet
of transformation, the clan's cloak of reason.
I am good when I am in motion,
when I think of myself at rest
in the knowledge of my moving,
when I have the vision of my mother at rest,
in moonlight, her lap the cradle of my father's head.
I am good when I trade my shells,
and walk from boundary to boundary,
unarmed and unafraid of another's speech.
I am good when I learn the world
through the touch of my present body.
I am good when I take the cove of a cub
                              into my care.
I am good when I hear the changes in my body
echo all my changes down the years,
when what I know indeed is what I would
                              know in deed.

I am good when I know the darkness of all light,
and accept the darkness, not as sign, but as my body.
This is the A of absolutes,
the logbook of judgments,
the good sign.

Pax

D.H. LAWRENCE

All that matters is to be one with the living God
to be a creature in the house of the God of Life.

Like a cat asleep on a chair
at peace, in peace
and at one with the master of the house, with the mistress,
at home, at home in the house of the living,
sleeping on the hearth, and yawning before the fire.

Sleeping on the hearth of the living world
yawning at home before the fire of life
feeling the presence of the living God
like a great reassurance
a deep calm in the heart
a presence
as of the master sitting at the board
in his own and greater being,
in the house of life.

Saint Francis and the Sow

GALWAY KINNELL

The bud
stands for all things,
even for those things that don't flower,
for everything flowers, from within, of self-blessing;
though sometimes it is necessary
to reteach a thing its loveliness,
to put a hand on its brow
of the flower
and retell it in words and in touch
it is lovely
until it flowers again from within, of self-blessing;
as Saint Francis
put his hand on the creased forehead
of the sow, and told her in words and in touch
blessings of earth on the sow, and the sow
began remembering all down her thick length,
from the earthen snout all the way
through the fodder and slops to the spiritual curl of the tail,
from the hard spininess spiked out from the spine
down through the great broken heart
to the sheer blue milken dreaminess spurting and shuddering
from the fourteen teats into the fourteen mouths sucking and
        blowing beneath them:
the long, perfect loveliness of sow.

The Flower

GEORGE HERBERT

How fresh, O Lord, how sweet and clean
Are thy returns! ev'n as the flowers in spring;
To which, besides their own demean,
The late-past frosts tributes of pleasure bring.
Grief melts away
Like snow in May,
As if there were no such cold thing.

Who would have thought my shrivel'd heart
Could have recover'd greenesse? It was gone
Quite under ground; as flowers depart
To see their mother-root, when they have blown;
Where they together
All the hard weather,
Dead to the world, keep house unknown.

These are thy wonders, Lord of power,
Killing and quickning, bringing down to hell
And up to heaven in an houre;
Making a chiming of a passing-bell.
We say amisse,
This or that is:
Thy word is all, if we could spell.

O that I once past changing were,
Fast in thy Paradise, where no flower can wither!
Many a spring I shoot up fair,
Offering at heav'n, growing and groning thither;
Nor doth my flower
Want a spring-showre,
My sinnes and I joining together.

But while I grow in a straight line,
Still upwards bent, as if heav'n were mine own,
Thy anger comes, and I decline:
What frost to that? what pole is not the zone,
Where all things burn,
When thou dost turn,
And the least frown of thine is shown?

And now in age I bud again,
After so many deaths I live and write;
I once more smell the dew and rain,
And relish versing: O my onely light,
It cannot be
That I am he
On whom thy tempests fell all night.

These are thy wonders, Lord of love,
To make us see we are but flowers that glide:
Which when we once can finde and prove,
Thou hast a garden for us, where to bide.
Who would be more,
Swelling through store,
Forfeit their Paradise by their pride.

The Windhover

To Christ our Lord

GERARD MANLEY HOPKINS

I caught this morning morning's minion, king-
    dom of daylight's dauphin, dapple-dawn-drawn Falcon, in his
       riding
Of the rolling level underneath him steady air, and striding
High there, how he rung upon the rein of a wimpling wing
In his ecstasy! then off, off forth on swing,
    As a skate's heel sweeps smooth on a bow-bend: the hurl and
      gliding
    Rebuffed the big wind. My heart in hiding
Stirred for a bird, – the achieve of, the mastery of the thing!

Brute beauty and valour and act, oh, air, pride, plume, here
    Buckle! AND the fire that breaks from thee then, a billion
Times told lovelier, more dangerous, O my chevalier!

    No wonder of it: shéer plód makes plough down sillion
Shine, and blue-bleak embers, ah my dear,
    Fall, gall themselves, and gash gold-vermilion.

Amber

TUA FORSSTRÖM

*translated from
the Finland Swedish
by* STINA KATCHADOURIAN

I have an amber ring that
shimmers through the lake's water

I dive, stir up the silt, particles
of minerals loosen and float along

the bottom, just like the oak-blossom bud's
starry hairs floated and were enclosed in the stone

then, during the time of sabre-toothed tigers
and small horses

in the sub-tropical forests with elderberry
and camphor trees here, where we live in houses

You see more clearly underwater
You see more clearly when you are sick

I dive into the cool water, stir up
silt, particles float slowly, minerals

like the oak-blossom bud's starry hairs float
in amber through thirty million years, shimmering

in the lake's water when I dive, everything
is stirred up, gets cloudy, shimmers

The Negro Speaks of Rivers

LANGSTON HUGHES

I've known rivers:
I've known rivers ancient as the world and older than the flow
      of human blood in human veins.

My soul has grown deep like the rivers.

I bathed in the Euphrates when dawns were young.
I built my hut near the Congo and it lulled me to sleep.
I looked upon the Nile and raised the pyramids above it.
I heard the singing of the Mississippi when Abe Lincoln went
      down to New Orleans, and I've seen its muddy bosom
      turn all golden in the sunset.

I've known rivers:
Ancient, dusky rivers.

My soul has grown deep like the rivers.

That's All?

ANNA HAJNAL

translated from the Hungarian
by JASCHA KESSLER

Shearing, as the gardener
snips the sucker,
controlling wild growth
with shaping hands,
looking and choosing –
which bud's to be the branch –
rooting out, cutting or pardoning
by design and scheme:
trimming pyramids, tall arches,
scissoring bowers for gods –
how I'd love doing that –
taking hold of the passionate growth
in my unmastered heart.

Slicing through wild, winding
trailers, charming
with a bright, sharp blade –
to but loosen its hold on me!

release its hold?
and must the clasper wither?
trailers, leaves, tendrils droop?
A French park, my loving?
moderation, cautious suffering?
precise forms, narrow blossoms,
the reign of geometry,
is my calmness to be a tight calmness?

The Myth
of the Twin

JOHN BURNSIDE

Say it moved when you moved:
a softness that rose in the ground
when you walked, or a give in your step,
the substance that Virgil saw
in the shadows under our feet;

and say it was out there, out in the snow,
meshed with the birdsong and light
the way things are real: a blackbird, a scribble of thorns,
a quickening into the moment, the present tense,

and the way that a stumbling or sudden
rooting in authenticity is not
the revelation of a foreign place,
but emptiness, a stillness in the frost,
the silence that stands in the birchwoods, the common soul.

Destruction

SHINKICHI
TAKAHASHI

translated from the Japanese
by LUCIEN STRYK
& TAKAHASHI IKEMOTO

The universe is forever falling apart –
No need to push the button,
It collapses at a finger's touch:
Why, it barely hangs on the tail of a sparrow's eye.

The universe is so much eye secretion,
Hordes leap from the tips
Of your nostril hairs. Lift your right hand:
It's in your palm. There's room enough
On the sparrow's eyelash for the whole.

A paltry thing, the universe:
Here is all strength, here the greatest strength.
You and the sparrow are one
And, should he wish, he can crush you.
The universe trembles before him.

9. INNER LIGHT

The Same Inside

ANNA SWIR

translated from the Polish
by CZESŁAW MIŁOSZ
& LEONARD NATHAN

Walking to your place for a love feast
I saw at a street corner
an old beggar woman.

I took her hand,
kissed her delicate cheek,
we talked, she was
the same inside as I am,
from the same kind,
I sensed this instantly
as a dog knows by scent
another dog.

I gave her money.
I could not part from her.
After all, one needs
someone who is close.

And then I no longer knew
why I was walking to your place.

Miranda on the Tube

DAVID CONSTANTINE

An empty carriage – or nearly, there was a girl –
We all piled in, bigger than usual,
And sprawled or hung and the first strange thing
Was how we had kept our distance and left her space,
And then it stopped. I ask you: nowadays
Who stares like that? No man who wants his face
Leaving alone and certainly never a girl

Who's normal, but we flick our eyes at a face
And off again before the owner comes
Or stare a girl to the floor, but there between
Stations halted, a nightmare for a girl,
She stared at us, at every one of us
In turn and all together and the strangest thing
Was this: she thought us beautiful, it showed

Like an open flower, it shone, it seemed her eyes
Were hands already learning over us
The human, the phenomenal, incredulous.
O faces soft as roses! We reviewed
Our boots, the worst came up in everyone
Like puke, out of the heart, our mouths were full
Of reason upon reason why we should not be

Looked at as though we were beautiful by her
A total stranger halted nowhere near
Help and wanting none. A carriage comes
Empty almost never and a girl alone
Never who looks like that. I sometimes see
A face a bit like hers: it hangs between
The smashed-up stations, sad as a bag-lady's.

The Bright Field

R.S. THOMAS

I have seen the sun break through
to illuminate a small field
for a while, and gone my way
and forgotten it. But that was the pearl
of great price, the one field that had
the treasure in it. I realise now
that I must give all that I have
to possess it. Life is not hurrying

on to a receding future, nor hankering after
an imagined past. It is the turning
aside like Moses to the miracle
of the lit bush, to a brightness
that seemed as transitory as your youth
once, but is the eternity that awaits you.

Tree

JANE HIRSHFIELD

It is foolish
to let a young redwood
grow next to a house.

Even in this
one lifetime,
you will have to choose.

That great calm being,
this clutter of soup pots and books –

Already the first branch-tips brush at the window.
Softly, calmly, immensity taps at your life.

To That Which Is Most Important

ANNA SWIR

translated from the Polish
by CZESŁAW MIŁOSZ
& LEONARD NATHAN

Were I able to shut
my eyes, ears, legs, hands
and walk into myself
for a thousand years,
perhaps I would reach
– I do not know its name –
what matters most.

'I stepped from Plank to Plank...'

EMILY DICKINSON

I stepped from Plank to Plank
A slow and cautious way
The Stars about my Head I felt
About my Feet the Sea.

I knew not but the next
Would be my final inch –
This gave me that precarious Gait
Some call Experience.

Variation on a Theme by Rilke

DENISE LEVERTOV

*(The Book of Hours,
Book 1, Poem 1, Stanza 1)*

A certain day became a presence to me;
there it was, confronting me – a sky, air, light:
a being. And before it started to descend
from the height of noon, it leaned over
and struck my shoulder as if with
the flat of a sword, granting me
honor and a task. The day's blow
rang out, metallic or it was I, a bell awakened,
and what I heard was my whole self
saying and singing what it knew: *I can.*

A Walk

RAINER MARIA RILKE

*translated from the German
by* ROBERT BLY

[Muzot, March 1924]

My eyes already touch the sunny hill,
going far ahead of the road I have begun.
So we are grasped by what we cannot grasp;
it has its inner light, even from a distance –

and changes us, even if we do not reach it,
into something else, which, hardly sensing it, we already are;
a gesture waves us on, answering our own wave...
but what we feel is the wind in our faces.

'Although the wind...'

Although the wind
blows terribly here,
the moonlight also leaks
between the roof planks
of this ruined house.

IZUMI SHIKIBU

translated from the Japanese
by JANE HIRSHFIELD
with MARIKO ARATANI

On the Treasury of the True Dharma Eye

Midnight. No waves,
no wind, the empty boat
is flooded with moonlight.

DOGEN

translated from the Japanese
by STEPHEN MITCHELL

'The soul, like the moon...'

LAL DED

*translated from the Kashmiri
by* COLEMAN BARKS

The soul, like the moon,
is new, and always new again.

And I have seen the ocean
continuously creating.

Since I scoured my mind
and my body, I too, Lalla,
am new, each moment new.

My teacher told me one thing,
Live in the soul.

When that was so,
I began to go naked,
and dance.

The Time Before Death

KABIR

translated from the Hindi
by ROBERT BLY

Friend, hope for the Guest while you are alive.
Jump into experience while you are alive!
Think…and think…while you are alive.
What you call 'salvation' belongs to the time before death.

If you don't break your ropes while you're alive,
do you think
ghosts will do it after?

The idea that the soul will join with the ecstatic
just because the body is rotten –
that is all fantasy.
What is found now is found then.
If you find nothing now,
you will simply end up with an apartment in the City of Death.
If you make love with the divine now, in the next life you will
        have the face of satisfied desire.

So plunge into the truth, find out who the Teacher is,
        Believe in the Great Sound!

Kabir says this: When the Guest is being searched for, it is the
        intensity of the longing for the Guest that does all the
        work.
Look at me, and you will see a slave of that intensity.

The Saying

ERNST STADLER

version from the German
by STEPHEN BERG

In an old book
I stumbled across a saying.
It was like a stranger
punching me in the face,

it won't stop
gnawing at me.
When I walk around at night,
looking for a beautiful girl,

when a lie or a description
of life or somebody's fake
way of being with people
occurs instead of reality,

when I betray myself with
an easy explanation
as if what's dark is clear,
as if life doesn't have thousands

of locked, burning gates,
when I use words without really
having known their strict openness
and put my hands around things

that don't excite me,
when a dream hides my face with soft hands
and the day avoids me,
cut off from the world,

cut off from who I am deeply,
I freeze where I am
and see hanging in the air in front of me
STOP BEING A GHOST!

The Eclipse

RICHARD EBERHART

I stood out in the open cold
To see the essence of the eclipse
Which was its perfect darkness.

I stood in the cold on the porch
And could not think of anything so perfect
As man's hope of light in the face of darkness.

The End of a Season

DANA GIOIA

I wanted to tell you how I walked tonight
down the hillside to the lake
after the storm had blown away
and say how everything suddenly seemed so clear
against the sparkling, rain-soaked streets
cold and bright as starlight.

I wanted to wake you up, despite the hour,
and drag you out into the dark
crisp air to feel the end of winter,
the cold we cursed so long
slipping away – and suddenly so precious
now that it was leaving.

But there is no one to come back to now,
only the night, its wind and rain, the chill
magnificence of its borrowed light,
the touch of this impossible season.

'Upon a gloomy night...'

(Song of the soul in rapture at having arrived at the height of perfection, which is union with God by the road of spiritual negation)

ST JOHN OF THE CROSS

translated from the Spanish by ROY CAMPBELL

Upon a gloomy night,
With all my cares to loving ardours flushed,
(O venture of delight!)
With nobody is sight
I went abroad when all my house was hushed.

In safety, in disguise,
In darkness up the secret stair I crept,
(O happy enterprise)
Concealed from other eyes
When all my house at length in silence slept.

Upon that lucky night
In secrecy, inscrutable to sight,
I went without discerning
And with no other light
Except for that which in my heart was burning.

It lit and led me through
More certain than the light of noonday clear
To where One waited near
Whose presence well I knew,
There where no other presence might appear.

Oh night that was my guide!
Oh darkness dearer than the morning's pride,
Oh night that joined the lover
To the beloved bride
Transfiguring them each into the other.

Within my flowering breast
Which only for himself entire I save
He sank into his rest
And all my gifts I gave
Lulled by the airs with which the cedars wave.

Over the ramparts fanned
While the fresh wind was fluttering his tresses,
With his serenest hand
My neck he wounded, and
Suspended every sense with its caresses.

Lost to myself I stayed
My face upon my lover having laid
From all endeavour ceasing:
And all my cares releasing
Threw them amongst the lilies there to fade.

Presences

ZOÉ KARÉLLI

translated from the Greek
by KIMON FRIAR

You must remain very much alone,
– quietness of the fragile movement,
anxiety of perception –
that the presences may come.

Do not be afraid,
the dead never die;
even the most humble and forgotten
exist, and when you are very much alone
they come near you
invested with the mystic silence
of the ineradicable,
the incomparable presence of man.

'Last night while I was sleeping'

ANTONIO MACHADO

translated from the Spanish
by WILLIS BARNSTONE

Last night while I was sleeping
I dreamed – blessed illusion! –
a fountain flowed
inside my heart.
Water, tell me by what hidden
channel you came to me
with a spring of new life
I never drank?

Last night while I was sleeping
I dreamed – blessed illusion! –
I had a beehive
inside my heart,
and from my old bitterness
the gold bees
were contriving white combs
and sweet honey.

Last night while I was sleeping
I dreamed – blessed illusion! –
a fiery sun glowed
inside my heart.
It was fiery, giving off heat
from a red fireplace.
It was the sun throwing out light
and made one weep.

Last night while I was sleeping
I dreamed – blessed illusion! –
that it was God I held
inside my heart.

Poem

KEITH ALTHAUS

The letter
the night
writes to you
with the last drop
of dreams,
(unfinished sentences
disappearing
on crumbling paper)
is addressed
to a grave,
a hole in the ground
where shovels
scoop debris
from past to future,
and the present
is blown away
like the dust
you breathed
standing in a cloud
watching in the rubble
the boundary stones
of your life removed.

Reconciliation

ELSE LASKER-SCHÜLER

translated from the German
by ROBERT ALTER

A great star has fallen into my lap...
We want to wake through the night,

To pray in languages
Notched like harps.

We want to be reconciled with the night
God overflows so much.

Our hearts are children,
They may rest tiredsweet.

And our lips want to kiss,
Why do you hesitate?

Do not join my heart to yours –
Always your blood reddens my cheeks.

We want to be reconciled with the night,
When we embrace, we do not die.

A great star has fallen into my lap.

Words

SHINKICHI TAKAHASHI

translated from the Japanese
by LUCIEN STRYK
& TAKAHASHI IKEMOTO

I don't take your words
Merely as words.
Far from it.

I listen
To what makes you talk —
Whatever that is —
And me listen.

FROM
Proverbs and Songs

ANTONIO MACHADO

translated from the Spanish
by WILLIS BARNSTONE

Between living and dream
there is a third way.
Guess it.

'If you look for the truth outside yourself'

TUNG-SHAN

translated from the Chinese
by STEPHEN MITCHELL

If you look for the truth outside yourself,
it gets farther and farther away.
Today walking alone,
I meet him everywhere I step.
He is the same as me,
yet I am not him.
Only if you understand it in this way
will you merge with the way things are.

Whoever grasps

**RAINER MARIA
RILKE**

*translated from the German
by* ROBERT BLY

Whoever grasps the thousand contradictions of his life,
pulls them together into a single image, that man, joyful
and thankful, drives the rioters out of the palace,
becomes celebratory in a *different* way, and you are the guest
whom he receives on the quiet evenings.

You are the second person in his solitude,
the tranquil hub of his talking with himself;
and every circle he draws around you
lifts him out of time on those compass legs.

'In all ten directions of the universe...'

RYOKAN

translated from the Japanese by STEPHEN MITCHELL

In all ten directions of the universe,
there is only one truth.
When we see clearly, the great teachings are the same.
What can ever be lost? What can be attained?
If we attain something, it was there from the beginning of time.
If we lose something, it is hiding somewhere near us.
Look: this ball in my pocket:
can you see how priceless it is?

Eternity

He who binds himself a joy
Does the winged life destroy;
But he who kisses the joy as it flies
Lives in eternity's sunrise.

WILLIAM BLAKE

Notes on the poets

Born in New Zealand in 1934, **Fleur Adcock** came to Britain in 1963. She writes about men and women, childhood, identity, roots and rootlessness, memory and loss as well as our interactions with nature and place. Her poised, ironic poems are remarkable for their wry wit, conversational tone and psychological insight, unmasking the deceptions of love or unravelling family lives.

Anna Akhmatova (1889-1966) was Russia's greatest modern poet. She was persecuted for much of her life and unable to publish her poetry during the Stalin years. Writing nothing down, she memorised all her work, and so survived, the people's conscience, the one who kept 'the great Russian word' alive.

Gillian Allnutt (*b.* 1949) is a highly individual English writer. Her meditative poems are both serious and light in touch, deeply humane and spiritually profound, 'earning their hard-won spiritual insights and flaring with sudden illuminations that are sustaining for all of us' (Michael Laskey).

Keith Althaus (*b.* 1945) is a neglected American poet who writes in a style both plain and rich. His conversational poems are philosophical in spirit, persistently enquiring after what a person can know and showing how insight into everyday life can transform the world. They take us into numinous territory we didn't know was there.

Maya Angelou (*b.* 1928) is one of the most celebrated African American writers. A poet, historian, songwriter, playwright, dancer, stage and screen producer, director, performer, singer and civil rights activist, best-known for her autobiographical books including *I Know Why the Caged Bird Sings*, she wrote and delivered a poem ('On the Pulse of the Morning') for President Bill Clinton's inauguration in 1993.

Chairil Anwar (1922-49) was a rebellious Indonesian writer who fought against Dutch colonial rule. He died at only 27 but his work had a lasting influence on post-independence poetry and prose. He released Indonesian poetry from the bonds of traditional forms and language, and his idealistic challenge, 'I want to live another thousand years', made him a cultural icon. This poem 'Me' (also known as 'Aku') was chanted in public rallies and other protests as a declaration of rebellion.

Wendell Berry (*b.* 1934) is an American poet as well as a conservationist and farmer in his native Kentucky. In *Standing by Words*, he writes: 'The imagination is our way to the Divine imagination, permitting us to see wholly – as whole and holy – what we perceive as scattered, as order what we perceive as random.'

John Berryman (1914–72) was a boldly original and innovative American poet, one of the "founders" of the so-called Confessional "school". His best-known and most imitated work is his series of sonnet-like *Dream Songs*, nearly 400 in number, a wild mixture of high lyricism and low comedy plumbing the extreme reaches of a human soul and psyche.

William Blake (1757-1827) is much celebrated now as a great English poet and artist, but his work was little-known in his lifetime. Blake was an apocalyptic visionary and a fiercely independent thinker – both profound and naïve – who resisted the narrow orthodoxies of his age. His *Songs of Innocence and of Experience* (1794) contrasts pastoral innocence and childhood with adult corruption and repression.

Robert Bly (*b.* 1926) is a highly influential American writer, poet, editor, translator, storyteller and father of 'the expressive men's movement'. His numerous books include *Iron John: A Book About Men* (1990) and the bestselling anthologies *The Rag and Bone Shop of the Heart* (1992) and *The Soul Is Here for Its Own Joy* (1995), a collection of sacred poetry from many cultures.

John Burnside (*b.* 1955) is a Scottish writer of radiant, meditative poetry and dark, brooding fiction. His books include several collections of poetry and one of short stories, several novels, and a memoir, *A Lie About My Father* (2006). In his essay in *Strong Words* (2000), he wrote: 'Our response to the world is essentially one of wonder, confronting the mysterious with a sense, not of being small, or insignificant, but of being part of a rich and complex narrative.'

Nina Cassian (*b.* 1924) is a Romanian poet, journalist and classical composer. She was granted asylum in the US when a friend was arrested by the Securitate in 1985 for possessing a diary including poems by her satirising the Ceausescu régime. Her poetry is highly personal and courageous, with passion as its central concern: passion as desire and passion as suffering. She believes that poetry 'is not to transcend life or to transform it, but it *is* life…Art is as alive as an animal.'

Paul Celan was born Paul Antschel in Romania in 1920 to German-speaking Jewish parents who later perished in Nazi death camps. Surviving a forced labour camp, he eventually settled in Paris. He wrote his poetry in German, and became one of the major writers of the Holocaust, committing suicide in 1970 by jumping from a bridge into the Seine. His work is characterised by a sense of horror, a belief that poetry must be open to the unexpected and unpredictable, and by his search for a redefinition of reality. In 1958 Celan said in a speech: 'A poem, as a manifestation of language and thus essentially dialogue, can be a message in a bottle, sent out in the – not always greatly hopeful – belief that somewhere and sometime it could wash up on land, on heartland perhaps.'

Chuang-tzu (369?-286? BCE) was a Chinese Taoist master, philosopher and comedian, celebrated as much for his work as a famous dream he described. He dreamed he was a butterfly but on waking didn't know if he was Chuang-tzu who'd just dreamt he was a butterfly or a butterfly now dreaming he was Chuang-tzu.

David Constantine (b. 1944) is an English poet known also for his translations of poets such as Enzensberger, Goethe, Hölderlin and Jaccottet. Like the work of the European poets who have nourished him, his poetry is informed by a profoundly humane vision of the world. His poems hold a worried and restless balance between celebration and anxiety, restraint and longing.

Imtiaz Dharker is a poet, artist and documentary film-maker. Her cultural experience spans three countries: born in Pakistan in 1954, she grew up a Muslim Calvinist in Glasgow, later eloping with a Hindu Indian to live in Bombay. She now lives between India and Britain, drawing her main themes from a life of transitions: childhood, exile, journeying, home, religious strife and terror.

Emily Dickinson (1830-86) lived for most of her life as a relative recluse in her lawyer father's house in Amherst, Massachusetts. She is said to have written 1,789 poems, only a handful of which were published – anonymously, by her friends – in her lifetime. Her fame grew quickly when posthumous editions of her work started appearing, the first in 1890, but editors could not resist interfering with her unconventional poems, changing words, punctuation and metre, and the first authoritative edition – with the poems printed as she wrote them – was not published until 1955.

Dogen Kigen (1200-53), also known as Dogen Zenji, was a Japanese Zen master, a philosopher, poet and painter who founded the Soto Zen school in Japan. He said that 'to study Buddhism is to study the self... Enlightenment is like the moon reflected in the water'.

Carol Ann Duffy (*b.* 1955) is Britain's most popular contemporary poet. Her poetry combines wit and social criticism with compelling lyricism to explore women's lives, language and identity, time and change, love and loss. Her colloquial dramatic monologues present unsettling slants on contemporary society, often by reinventing myths and fairytales.

Richard Eberhart (1904-2005) was an inspirational American poet concerned with transcending experience to connect with a unifying life force. 'My poetry celebrates life,' he wrote, 'which does not last long, and mankind, which is temporal as well, through understanding and perception of my times...'

Fiona Farrell (*b.* 1947) is a New Zealand poet better known for her fiction and plays. Her energetic and highly varied writing has two central themes: a concern with separateness, with how society judges and deals with difference in belief or appearance or behaviour; and the opposite: the possibility of personal emancipation through the apparently miraculous transformation of the mundane.

Edward Field (*b.* 1924) is an American poet often linked with the Beats, also known for his translations of Eskimo songs and stories. Immediate, funny and completely personal, his poems are small essays on the human condition. He gives a frank account of New York's postwar literary and gay culture in his memoir *The Man Who*

Would Marry Susan Sontag and Other Intimate Literary Portraits of the Bohemian Era (2006).

Carolyn Forché (*b.* 1951) is a visionary American writer whose poetry combines political engagement and spiritual awareness. Born in Detroit of Czech-American parentage, she describes herself as a 'junkheap Catholic' perennially drawn to issues of social justice. She has devoted her life and work to exposing tyranny and bearing witness to the atrocities of modern times. Her books include four collections, *Gathering the Tribes* (1976), *The Country Between Us* (1981), *The Angel of History* (1994) and *Blue Hour* (2003), and an anthology *Against Forgetting: Twentieth-Century Poetry of Witness* (1993).

Tua Forsström (*b.* 1947) is a visionary Finland-Swedish writer who has become Finland's most celebrated contemporary poet. Her poetry draws its sonorous and plangent music from the landscapes of Finland, seeking harmony between the troubled human heart and the threatened natural world.

Robert Frost (1874–1963) was the most popular American poet of the 20th century, known especially for his 'Stopping by Woods on a Snowy Evening' and for 'The Road Not Taken', voted America's favourite modern poem. Most of his best-known poems are set in the New Hampshire farmland where he lived. Joseph Brodsky said of Frost (1996): 'He is generally regarded as the poet of the countryside, of rural settings – as a folksy, crusty, wisecracking old gentleman farmer, generally of positive disposition. In short, as American as apple pie...Now, this is obviously a romantic caricature...Nature, for this poet, is neither friend nor foe, nor is it the backdrop for human drama; it is this poet's terrifying self-portrait.'

Dana Gioia (*b.* 1950) is an American writer of Italian and Mexican descent. A leading New Formalist poet, he is also a critic and outspoken literary commentator, with books including the controversial *Can Poetry Matter?* (1992), and Chairman of the National Endowment for the Arts. His highly musical poetry is quietly visionary, often showing human lives rooted in the natural world.

John Glenday (*b.* 1952) is an unjustly neglected Scottish poet who has worked as a psychiatric nurse and as an addictions counsellor. 'Glenday is a kind of practical mystic and has been writing poems of quite spiritual power for many years now, but is only starting to get the recognition he has almost studiously avoided. Glenday's subject is the soul and the soul of things' (Don Paterson).

Johann Wolfgang von Goethe (1749-1832) was a German polymath: a poet, novelist, dramatist, philosopher, scientist and painter, as well as a minister for the duchy of Weimar. Best-known for his verse drama *Faust*, he is one of the greatest figures in Western literature.

Anna Hajnal (1907-77) was a Hungarian writer whose poetry was changed by war and Communism. Originally a poet of love-ecstasy, she was constrained by socialist realism for many years. Her later work was inspired by war, plants, folk-poetry and primitive cultures.

Thich Nhat Hanh (*b.* 1926) is an exiled Vietnamese Buddhist monk and peace activist who lives in the retreat community of Plum Village in south-west France which he founded. A tireless worker for peace during the Vietnam War, he became an internationally renowned spiritual guide and has written more than 75 books of prose poetry, and prayers.

Kerry Hardie (*b.* 1951) is an Irish writer who has published four books of poetry and two novels. Often following the annual round of rural life, her poetry explores the mystery of 'why we are here'. 'In many of these poems, illness opens into a compassionate understanding of suffering and death, familial and historical …she finds in nature a redemptive power for the body, prompting the big questions of human and divine purpose' (Selina Guinness).

Joy Harjo (*b.* 1951) is a Native American poet and storyteller. Influenced not only by her own Muscogee (Creek) traditions but also by the Navajo Beauty Way and by Pueblo stories, her work is grounded in her relationship with the earth on a physical, spiritual and mythopoetic level. She is also a multi-talented performer and saxophonist, combining poetry and chanting with tribal music, jazz, funk and rock.

Kaylin Haught was born in Illinois in 1947, and grew up in Oklahoma, where her father was an oil-field worker and part-time preacher and her mother a housewife and part-time factory worker. She now lives in Texas, where she writes: 'Poetry is my life, my joy, my work.'

George Herbert (1593-1633) was, with John Donne, the most significant English Metaphysical poet of the 17th century. A much esteemed Cambridge scholar, he was briefly an MP, and for the last three years of his life a parish priest in Wiltshire. Unpublished at his death, his collection *The Temple* became one of most most loved volumes of English religious poetry.

Jane Hirshfield (*b.* 1953) is a visionary American poet who trained as a Zen Buddhist. Both sensual meditations and passionate investigations, her poems reveal complex truths in language luminous and precise. Her books include *The Ink Dark Moon: Love Poems by Ono no Komachi and Izumi Shikibu, Women of the Ancient Court of Japan* (1988), *Women in Praise of the Sacred: 43 Centuries of Spiritual Poetry by Women* (1994), *Each Happiness Ringed by Lions: Selected Poems* (2005) and *After* (2006).

Gerard Manley Hopkins (1844-89) was a major poet of the Victorian period. An English Jesuit priest, he was virtually unknown as a writer in his lifetime. His highly original poetry – notable for its musicality and innovative "sprung rhythm" – was not published until 1918, many years after his death.

Marie Howe (*b*. 1950) is an American poet who has published two collections and co-edited *In the Company of My Solitude: American Writing from the AIDS Pandemic* (1994). Her poetry explores the themes of relationship, attachment and loss in a personal search for transcendence.

Langston Hughes (1902-67) was the leading African American writer in the Harlem Renaissance of the 1920s. A poet, novelist, short story writer and dramatist, he was known for his vivid portrayals of black life in America as well as for his engagement with the world of jazz.

Cynthia Huntington (*b*. 1952) is an American writer who has published three collections and a prose memoir, *The Salt House*. Treating suffering and loss with unusual clarity and wisdom, 'hers is a poetry of wit, surprise, observation, and exemplary intelligence' (Donald Hall).

Ikkyu (1394-1481) was an eccentric, iconoclastic Japanese Zen Buddhist priest, poet and flute-player, and one of the creators of the formal Japanese tea ceremony.

Born in England, **M.K. Joseph** (1914-81) was a leading New Zealand poet whose work was strongly influenced by fighting in the Second World War. His elegant poetry confronts 'the moral complexities of cruelty and mercy, apocalypse and hope, based in, but not constrained by his Catholic faith' (Roger Robinson).

Kabir (1440-1518) was an illiterate Indian mystic, a poet, weaver and disciple of Ramananda who spent most of his life in a tiny shop in Benares. His poems have been passed down as songs through many generations and are still popular in India. Revered by both Hindus and Muslims, his name means 'Great One' in Arabic.

Anna Kamienska (1920-86) was a prominent member of the Polish literary generation who experienced the Second World War as young men and women. She became an important figure in postwar Polish literature, known for her novels, short stories, critical works and translations from several languages as well as for her poetry.

Estonia's **Jaan Kaplinski** (*b*. 1941) is one of Europe's major poets. Also a linguist, translator, sociologist and ecologist, he lectured on the history of Western civilisation at Tartu University and was a deputy of the Estonian Parliament for three years. His philosophical poetry shows the influence of European Modernism, classical Chinese poetry and Buddhist philosophy.

Zoé Karélli (1901-98) (Chryssoula Argiriadou) was one of foremost modern Greek poets of Thessalonia. She wrote passionately argued existential poetry, seeking personal meaning in a world of spiritual disintegration and feeling 'the burdensome love for an existence as it is tried and tested by the knowledge of death' (Kimon Friar).

Kapka Kassabova (*b*. 1973) is a Bulgarian émigré poet who writes in English but with a European imagination. Her well-travelled poems speak from different parts of the world and different moments of history, but they always speak of the many ways to be lost and disoriented: in a place, in the past, in fear, in love, in the very quickness of life.

X.J. Kennedy (*b*. 1929) is a versatile American formalist poet, best known for his light verse and his 'Brats' series of dark poetry for children. Irked by the hardship of having the name of Joseph Kennedy, he stuck the X on and has been stuck with it ever since.

Brendan Kennelly (*b.* 1936) is Ireland's most popular modern poet. His poem 'Begin' was widely circulated by Irish Americans in the aftermath of 9/11. 'His poems shine with the wisdom of somebody who has thought deeply about the paradoxical strangeness and familiarity and wonder of life' (Sister Stanislaus Kennedy).

Jane Kenyon (1947-95) was an American poet who fought depression and other illnesses for much of her life. Her quietly musical poems are compassionate meditations intently probing the life of the heart and spirit. Observing and absorbing small miracles in everyday life, they grapple with fundamental questions of human existence.

Galway Kinnell (*b.* 1927) is an American poet whose diverse work ranges from odes of kinship with nature to realistic evocations of urban life, from religious quest to political statement, from brief imagistic lyrics to extended, complex meditations. He is 'America's pre-eminent visionary', and his poetry 'greets each new age with rapture and abundance [and] sets him at the table with his mentors: Rilke, Whitman, Frost' (National Book Award citation, 2003).

Stanley Kunitz (1905-2006) was a highly influential American poet, editor, translator and teacher committed to fostering community amongst artists. His poetry is autobiographical but also fiercely visionary. Drawing on Jungian symbolism, he engaged with personal tragedy and public conscience to produce a resilient poetry of testing wisdom.

Lal Ded (Mother Lalla or Lalleshwari) was a 14th-century mystic seer, the first in a long list of saints preaching the medieval mysticism which spread throughout India. Married at 12, she later escaped her husband and abusive mother-in-law to become a wandering ascetic, singing of her bliss and love for the Divine, her followers including Hindus as well as Muslims. The Kashmiri language is full of her many wise sayings.

Else Lasker-Schüler (1869-1945) was a leading German Expressionist poet, known especially for her love poetry, religious poems and prayers, much of it rich in Biblical and oriental motifs. She fled to Switzerland after being attacked by Nazi thugs, and lived throughout the war in Palestine, where she died in poverty. She is buried on the Mount of Olives in Jerusalem.

D.H. Lawrence (1885-1930) was one of the major English writers of the 20th century, a controversial novelist as well as a visionary poet who saw his verse as 'direct utterance from the instant, whole man'. 'The living movement of Lawrence's poetry best conveys his gospel of sensory "life": a gospel that has both rejected and absorbed the non-conformist religion in which he was reared' (Edna Longley).

Denise Levertov (1923-97), one of the 20th century's foremost American poets, was born in England, the daughter of a Russian Jewish scholar turned Anglican priest and a Welsh Congregationalist mother, both parents descended from mystics. 'Meditative and evocative, Levertov's poetry concerns itself with the search for meaning. She sees the poet's role as a priestly one; the poet is the mediator between ordinary people and the divine mysteries' (Susan J. Zeuenbergen).

Antonio Machado y Ruiz (1875-1939) was Spain's most popular modern poet and a leading figure in the intellectual movement known as the Generation of '98 who sought the political and cultural revitalisation of Spain. His is a poetry of time and memory, filled with philosophical melancholy and often evoking the stony landscapes and diminished glories of his homeland.

Thomas Merton (1915-68) was a writer and Trappist monk at Our Lady of Gethsemani Abbey in Kentucky. Probably the most influential American Catholic author of the 20th century, he became deeply interested in Asian religions, particularly Zen Buddhism, and in promoting East-West dialogue. As well as poetry, his writings include an autobiography, *The Seven Storey Mountain*, and such classics as *New Seeds of Contemplation* and *Zen and the Birds of Appetite*.

Czesław Miłosz (1911-2004) was Poland's foremost modern poet, often described as a poet of memory and witness. Born in Lithuania (then ruled by Tsarist Russia), he worked for underground presses in Nazi-occupied Warsaw, later becoming a diplomat and given political asylum in France in 1951. He received the Nobel Prize in Literature in 1980.

Kenji Miyazawa (1896-1933) died at 37 from tuberculosis. Little known in his lifetime, he became a much loved children's author now regarded as Japan's greatest poet of the 20th century. Influenced by Buddhism and by his strong personal identification with nature, many of his poems and tales are set in the remote prefecture of Iwate, where he travelled from village to village, teaching the science of rice cultivation.

Portia Nelson (1920-2001) was an American singer, author, actress and composer whose film roles included Sister Berthe in *The Sound of Music*. This poem has achieved wide fame beyond her inspirational book *There's a Hole in My Sidewalk: The Romance of Self-Discovery*.

Naomi Shihab Nye is an American writer, anthologist, educator and 'wandering poet'. Born in 1952 to a Palestinian father and an American mother, she has published over 20 books. She gives voice to her experience as an Arab-American through poems about heritage and peace that overflow with a humanitarian spirit.

Dennis O'Driscoll (*b*. 1954) is an Irish poet, critic and anthologist who has worked as a civil servant since the age of 16. He is a poet of humanity whose wittily observant poetry is attuned to the tragedies and comedies of contemporary life. His books include *Troubled Thoughts, Majestic Dreams: Selected Prose Writings* (2001), *New & Selected Poems* (2004) and *The Bloodaxe Book of Poetry Quotations* (2006).

Mary Oliver (*b*. 1935) is one of America's best-loved poets. Her luminous poetry celebrates nature and beauty, love and the spirit, silence and wonder, extending the visionary American tradition of Whitman, Emerson and Emily Dickinson. It is nourished by her intimate knowledge and minute daily observation of the New England coast around Cape Cod, its woods and ponds, its birds, animals, plants and trees. Her many books include *Wild Geese: Selected Poems* (2004) and *Thirst* (2007).

Molly Peacock (*b*. 1947) is an American New Formalist poet and educator who lives in Toronto. She writes about love and sex with disarming frankness as well as on war, spirituality and family life. Her poetry confronts psychological truths with unflinching honesty.

Portugal's **Fernando Pessoa** (1888-1935) lived in Lisbon for most of his life, and died in obscurity there, but is now recognised as one of the most innovative and radical literary figures in modern poetry. He wrote under numerous "heteronyms", literary alter egos with their own identities and writing styles, who supported and criticised each other in the literary journals. The poem here was published by Pessoa as an ode by Ricardo Reis.

Amrita Pritam (1919-2005), the first prominent woman Punjabi poet and fiction writer, was known as the doyenne of Punjabi literature. Born to a Sikh family, she moved to India after partitition, and also wrote in Hindi and Urdu.

Rainer Maria Rilke (1875-1926) was one of the greatest poets of the 20th century. His poetry addresses questions of how to live and relate to the world in a voice that is simultaneously prophetic and intensely personal. Most of his major work was written in German, including the *Duino Elegies* and *Sonnets to Orpheus*. Born in Prague, he lived in France from 1902 and then Switzerland from 1919 until his death.

Jelaluddin Rumi (1207-73) was a Sufi mystic and poet, born in what is now Afghanistan, who founded the ecstatic dancing order known as the Mevlevi or Whirling Dervishes. Rumi would recite his poems in any place, sometimes day and night for several days, with his disciple Husam writing them down.

Ryokan (1758-1831) was a Japanese Zen master, calligrapher and poet-monk, and one of the most beloved figures in Japanese literature.

St John of the Cross (1542-91) (Juan de la Cruz) was a major figure in the Catholic Reformation, a Spanish mystic and Carmelite friar. His poetry and writings on the growth of the soul (in the Christian sense of detachment from creatures and attachment to God) are considered the summit of mystical Spanish literature.

David Scott (*b*. 1947) is an English Anglican priest whose compassionate poetry achieves resonance through careful observation and quiet understatement. Springing from ordinary events or an aspect of the priestly life, they work up a detail into a moment of significance.

Masaoka Tsunenori Shiki (1867-1902) was one of Japan's greatest modern writers, credited with modernising Japan's two traditional verse forms, haiku and tanka.

Izumi Shikibu (974?-1034?) was one of the predominant geniuses of the Heian court of imperial Japan, and the outstanding woman poet of Japanese literature. 'This poem's power and resonance emerge when one reads it as a Buddhist statement: it is in the midst of poverty and suffering that the moonlight of enlightenment is able to enter the human heart' (Jane Hirshfield).

Edith Södergran (1892-1923) is now regarded as Finland's greatest modern poet, a mystic modernist whose startlingly original poetry (written in Swedish) transcends the limits imposed by her lifelong struggle against TB. But when she died in poverty at 31, Södergran had been dismissed as a mad, megalomaniac aristocrat by most of her Finnish contemporaries.

Ernst Stadler (1883-1914) was a pioneer of German Expressionist poetry, which coupled angst and absurdity in disturbing visions of downfall and decay. Stadler put body images at the centre of many of his poems, especially evoking dancers, strumpets and statues. He served as an artillery lieutenant in the Germany army, and was killed on the Western Front at Ypres.

William Stafford (1914-93) was a much loved American poet. His contemplative poetry celebrates human virtues and universal mysteries, with nature, war, technology and Native American people as his abiding themes. In a typical Stafford poem he seeks an almost sacred place in the wilderness untouched by man, finding meaning in the quest itself and its implications.

Pauline Stainer (*b*. 1941) is an English poet 'working at the margins of the sacred' (John Burnside). Her poetry explores sacred myth, legend, history-in-landscape and human feeling – and their connections to the inner landscapes of the imaginative mind.

Susan Stewart (*b*. 1952) is an American poet and critic who teaches the history of poetry, aesthetics and the philosophy of literature at Princeton University. 'Investigating themes such as miniaturisation, giganticism, plagiarism, forgery, the souvenir, the collection, Stewart often makes strange and disorienting that which we usually take to be familiar and of common sense' (MacArthur Foundation citation).

Anna Swir (1909-84) (Anna Swirszczynska) was a popular Polish poet. She worked for the Polish Resistance during the war, nursing the wounded during the Warsaw uprising of 1944. An agnostic and militant feminist, she became known especially for her fierce poetry of love and war.

Wisława Szymborska (*b*. 1923) is Poland's foremost living poet. She won the Nobel Prize in Literature in 1996 'for poetry that with ironic precision allows the historical and biological context to come to light in fragments of human reality'. Her short poems are concerned with large existential issues, exploring the human condition with sceptical wit and ironic understatement.

Shinkichi Takahashi (1901-87) was Japan's foremost Zen poet of the 20th century, one of very few Japanese writers trained under a Zen master (Shizan Ashikaga). Takahashi was widely admired not just for his philosophy but for his freedom of imagination and his ability to address several subjects at the same time.

R.S. Thomas (1913-2000) was one of the major poets of our time as well as one of the finest religious poets in the English language and Wales's greatest poet. He was an Anglican priest, an isolated figure who worked in only three parishes over a lifetime. Most of his poetry covers ground he treads repeatedly: man and God, science and nature, time and history, the land and people of Wales.

Jean Toomer (1894-1967) was an American poet and novelist of mixed race descent and a key figure in the Harlem Renaissance of the 1920s. His best-known book is *Cane* (1923), written after experiencing life in the racially segregated South. His later work shows the influence of Gurdjieff's teachings and then of his shift into Quakerism.

Tung-shan Liang-chieh (807-69) was a Chinese Zen Master, the founder of the Ts'ao-Tung (Soto) school of Zen. His dialectical approach, which emphasised meditation whilst resisting the institutionalisation of any specific practice, sustained the idea of stages of enlightenment for more than three hundred years, until Dogen was struck by its depth and force and brought it to Japan as Soto Zen.

Chase Twichell (*b*. 1950) is an American poet and founder-editor of Ausable Press. She was a Zen Buddhist student of John Daido Loori at Zen Mountain Monastery in the Catskills and has said of her two disciplines: 'Zazen and poetry are both studies of the mind. I find the internal pressure exerted by emotion and by a koan to be similar in surprising and unpredictable ways. Zen is a wonderful sieve through which to pour a poem. It strains out whatever's inessential.'

César Vallejo (1892-1938) was an innovative Peruvian poet who published only three books of poetry in his lifetime, including the dramatically experimental *Trilce* (1922), a landmark in Latin American literature. Imprisoned after being blamed for an outbreak of violence, he left

Peru shortly afterwards in 1923, and spent the rest of his life in exile, mostly in poverty in France and Spain, where he embraced Marxism, espoused the Republican cause in the Spanish Civil War, and wrote revolutionary poetry incorporating war reportage.

David Wagoner (*b.* 1926) is an American poet and novelist known for his compassionate observation of both the natural and the human worlds. In a style by turns direct and intricate, he distils the essential emotions from people's encounters with each other, with nature and with themselves.

Derek Walcott (*b.* 1930) is not only the foremost Caribbean poet writing today (as well as a dramatist and painter) but a major figure in world literature, recognised with the award of the Nobel Prize in Literature in 1992 'for a poetic *œuvre* of great luminosity, sustained by a historical vision, the outcome of a multicultural commitment'. Most of his work explores the Caribbean cultural experience, the history, landscape and lives of its multiracial people, fusing folk culture and oral tales with the classical, avant-garde and English literary tradition.

James Wright (1927-80) was one of the most influential American poets of the 20th century. Whether drawing on his native Ohio, the natural world, or the luminous resonant Italy of his later work, his powerful yet vulnerable voice embraces many facets of human experience through shifting tones and moods, both lyric and ironic, autobiographical and social.

Jay Wright (*b.* 1935) has been a neglected figure in American poetry. His work is a quest for identity, setting the African American experience in a wider context of ritual, history and culture. He sees himself as an artist-spokesman for African Americans, Africans and Hispanics, dramatising historical and psychological continuities linking him with his ancestors.

Al Young (*b.* 1939) is an African American poet and novelist. Also a writer on jazz, he views the musical impulse as the beat of writing and the lifeblood of individual imagination. Young portrays the American experience as a world transcending divisive political, racial and cultural barriers.

We regret that we were unable to include poems by **Louise Glück** and **Mark Strand** in this anthology because Carcanet Press's conditions of use were unacceptable, but we are grateful to all the other publishers, authors and rights holders for their kindness and cooperation.

The original American spellings are retained in work by American poets and translators.

Acknowledgements

The poems in this anthology are reprinted from the following books, all by permission of the publishers listed unless stated otherwise. Thanks are due to all the copyright holders cited below for their kind permission:

Fleur Adcock: *Poems 1960-2000* (Bloodaxe Books, 2000). **Anna Akhmatova**: *The Complete Poems of Anna Akhmatova*, ed. & intr. Roberta Reeder, copyright © 1989, 1992, 1997 Judith Hemschemeyer, by permission of Zephyr Press. **Gillian Allnutt**: *How the Bicycle Shone: New & Selected Poems* (Bloodaxe Books, 2007). **Keith Althaus**: *Ladder of Hours: Poems 1969-2005*, copyright © 2005 Keith Althaus, by permission of Ausable Press, www. ausablepress.org. **Maya Angelou**: *The Complete Collected Poems* (Virago Press, 1994), by permission of the author and Little, Brown Book Group. **Chairil Anwar**: *The Voice of the Night: Complete Poetry and Prose of Chairil Anwar*, tr. Burton Raffel, by permission of Ohio University Press/ Swallow Press, Athens, Ohio (www.ohiou.edu/oupress).

    Wendell Berry: *The Selected Poems of Wendell Berry* (Counterpoint, USA, 1998), by permission of Counterpoint Press, a member of Perseus Books Group. **John Berryman**: *Collected Poems 1937-1971* (Farrar, Straus & Giroux, USA, 1989; Faber & Faber, 1990). **Robert Bly**: 'The Third Body' from *Loving a Woman in Two Worlds* (1985), copyright © 1985 Robert Bly, by permission of Doubleday, a division of Random House Inc. **John Burnside**: *The Myth of the Twin* (Jonathan Cape, 1994), by permission of the Random House Group Ltd.

    Nina Cassian: *Life Sentence: Selected Poems*, ed. William Jay Smith (Anvil Press Poetry, 1990). **Paul Celan**: 'Mandorla', 'Speak You Too' and 'Corona' from *Selected Poems and Prose of Paul Celan*, tr. John Felstiner (W.W. Norton & Company, 2000), copyright © 2001 John Felstiner, by permission of W.W. Norton & Company, Inc.; 'Mandorla' from Paul Celan, *Die Niemandsrose* © 1959 S. Fischer Verlag GmbH, Frankfurt am Main. **Chuang-tzu**: 'When the Shoe Fits', tr. Thomas Merton, from *Collected Poems of Thomas Merton* (New Directions, 1977), copyright © 1977 by the Trustees of the Merton Legacy trust, by kind permission of Pollinger Limited and the estate of Thomas Merton. **David Constantine**: *Collected Poems* (Bloodaxe Books, 2004). **Imtiaz Dharker**: *Postcards from god* (Bloodaxe Books, 1997). **Emily Dickinson**: by permission of the publishers and the Trustees of Amherst College from *The Poems of Emily Dickinson: Reading Edition*, Ralph W. Franklin, ed., Cambridge, Mass.: The Belknap Press of Harvard University Press, copyright © 1998 by the President and Fellows of Harvard College. Copyright © 1951, 1955, 1979, 1983 by the President and Fellows of Harvard College. **Dogen**: 'On the Treasury of the True Dharma Eye', tr. Stephen Mitchell, from *The Enlightened Heart: An Anthology of Sacred Poetry*, ed. Stephen Mitchell (HarperCollins, USA, 1989; HarperPerennial, 1993), copyright © 1989 Stephen Mitchell, by permission of HarperCollins Publishers. **Carol Ann Duffy**: *Mean Time* (Anvil Press Poetry, 1993).

    Richard Eberhart: *Collected Poems 1930-1976* (Replica Books, USA, 2001).

    Fiona Farrell: *The Inhabited Initial* (Auckland University Press, NZ, 1999). **Edward Field**: *Stand Up, Friend, With Me* (Grove Press Inc., NY, 1963), by permission of the author. **Carolyn Forché**: *Blue Hour* (HarperCollins, USA; Bloodaxe Books, UK, 2003). **Tua Forsström**: 'Amber', tr. Stina Katchadourian, from *I studied once at a wonderful faculty*, tr. David McDuff & Stina Katchadourian (Bloodaxe Books, 2006). **Robert Frost**: *The Poetry of Robert Frost*, ed. Edward Connery Lathem (Jonathan Cape, 1967), by permission of the Random House Group Ltd.

    Dana Gioia: *Daily Horoscope* (Graywolf Press, 1986), by permission of Graywolf Press, Saint Paul, Minnesota, USA. **John Glenday**: *Undark* (Peterloo Poets, 1995). **Johann Wolfgang von Goethe**: *Selected Poetry*, tr. David Luke (Libris, 1999), copyright © Estate of David Luke.

    Anna Hajnal: 'That's All?', tr. Jascha Kessler, first published in *The American Pen*, V: I (Spring 1973). **Thich Nhat Hanh**: *Call Me by My True Names: The Collected*

Poems of Thich Nhat Hanh (Parallax Press, USA, 1999). **Kerry Hardie:** *The Sky Didn't Fall* (Gallery Press, 2003), by permission of the author and the Gallery Press, Loughcrew, Oldcastle, County Meath, Ireland. **Joy Harjo:** *In Mad Love and War* (Wesleyan University Press, 1990), copyright © 1990 Joy Harjo, by permission of Wesleyan University Press. **Kaylin Haught:** 'God Says Yes to Me', first published in *The Palm of Your Hand*, ed. Steve Kowat (Tilbury House Publishers, USA, 1995), by permission of the author. **Jane Hirshfield:** 'The Weighing' and 'Tree' from *Each Happiness Ringed by Lions: Selected Poems* (Bloodaxe Books, 2005); 'Burlap Sack' from *After* (HarperCollins, USA; Bloodaxe Books, UK, 2006). **Marie Howe:** *What the Living Do* (W.W. Norton & Company, 1997), copyright © 1997 by Marie Howe, by permission of W.W. Norton & Company, Inc. **Langston Hughes:** *The Collected Poems of Langston Hughes* (Knopf, NY, 1994), by permission of David Higham Associates. **Cynthia Huntington:** *The Radiant* (Four Way Books, New York, 2003), copyright © 2003 Cynthia Huntington, by permission of Four Way Books Inc., all rights reserved.

Ikkyu: 'My real dwelling', from *Wild Ways: Zen Poems of Ikkyu*, tr. John Stevens (White Pine Press, USA, 2003).

M.K. Joseph: *Inscription on a Paper Dart: Selected Poems 1945-72* (Auckland University Press/Oxford University Press, NZ, 1974), by permission of Mrs M.J. Joseph and the estate of M.K. Joseph.

Kabir: *The Kabir Book*, tr. Robert Bly, copyright © 1971, 1977 Robert Bly, reprinted by permission of Visva-Bharati University Publishing Dept. **Anna Kamienska:** *Two Darknesses,* tr. Tomasz P. Krzeszowski & Desmond Graham (Flambard Press, 1994). **Jaan Kaplinski:** *Evening Brings Everything Back*, tr. Jaan Kaplinki with Fiona Sampson (Bloodaxe Books, 2004). **Zoé Karélli:** 'Presences', tr. Kimon Friar, copyright © 1978 Kimon Friar. **Kapka Kassabova:** *Someone else's life* (Bloodaxe Books, 2003). **X.J. Kennedy:** *The Lords of Misrule: Poems 1992-2001* (Johns Hopkins University Press, 2002), © 2002 X.J. Kennedy, by permission of The Johns Hopkins University Press. **Brendan Kennelly:** *Familiar Strangers: New & Selected Poems 1960-2004* (Bloodaxe Books, 2004). **Jane Kenyon:** *Let Evening Come: Selected Poems* (Bloodaxe Books, 2005), copyright © 2005 Estate of Jane Kenyon, from *Collected Poems* by permission of Graywolf Press, Saint Paul, Minnesota. **Galway Kinnell:** *Selected Poems* (Houghton Mifflin, USA, 2000; Bloodaxe Books, UK, 2001). **Stanley Kunitz:** *The Collected Poems* (W.W. Norton & Company, 2000), copyright © 2000 Stanley Kunitz, by permission of W.W. Norton & Company, Inc.

Lal Ded: 'The soul, like the moon...', from *Lalla: Naked Song*, tr. Coleman Barks (Maypop Books, USA, 1992), copyright © 1992 Coleman Barks, by permission of Maypop Books, 196 Westview Drive, Athens GA 30606, USA. **Else Lasker-Schüler:** Robert Alter for translation of 'Reconciliation' from *Gesammelte Werke in Drei Bänden, I: Gedichte 1902-1943* (Kösel, Munich, 1961), first published in English in *The Penguin Book of Women Poets* (1978). **D.H. Lawrence:** 'Demiurge' and 'Pax' both first published posthumously in *Last Poems* (1932), and reprinted from *Complete Poems*, ed. Vivian de Sola Pinto & Warren Roberts (Penguin, 1977). **Denise Levertov:** 'Living', from *The Sorrow Dance* (1967), and 'Talking to Grief', from *Life in the Forest* (1978), reprinted from *New Selected Poems* (New Directions, USA, 2002; Bloodaxe Books, UK, 2003) by permission of Bloodaxe Books Ltd; 'The Fountain' from *Poems 1960-1967* (New Directions, USA, 1967) and 'Variation on a Theme by Rilke' from *Breathing the Water* (New Directions, USA, 1987; Bloodaxe Books, UK, 1988) by permission of Pollinger Limited and the estate of Denise Levertov.

Antonio Machado: *Border of a Dream: Selected Poems*, tr. Willis Barnstone (Copper Canyon Press, USA, 2004), copyright © 2004 the Heirs of Antonio Machado, English translation copyright © 2004 Willis Barnstone, by permission of Copper Canyon Press, www.coppercanyonpress.org. **Thomas Merton:** 'Song for Nobody' and 'In Silence', from *Collected Poems of Thomas Merton* (New Directions, 1977), copyright © 1977 by the Trustees of the Merton Legacy trust, by kind permission of Pollinger Limited and the estate of Thomas Merton. **Czesław Miłosz:** *New &*

Collected Poems 1931-2001 (Allen Lane The Penguin Press, 2001), copyright © Czeslaw Milosz Royalties Inc., 1988, 1991, 1995, 2001. **Kenji Miyazawa:** *Strong in the Rain: Selected Poems*, tr. Roger Pulvers (Bloodaxe Books, 2007).

Portia Nelson: *There's a Hole in My Sidewalk* (Beyond Words Publishing, Inc., Hillsboro, Oregon USA, 1993). **Naomi Shihab Nye:** *Words under the Words: Selected Poems* (Far Corner Books, USA, 1995).

Dennis O'Driscoll: *New and Selected Poems* (Anvil Press Poetry, 2004). **Mary Oliver:** 'The Journey' and 'Wild Geese' from *Dream Work* (Grove/Atlantic, USA, 1986), by permission of Grove/Atlantic and the author; 'Some Questions You Might Ask' and 'The Summer Day' from *House of Light* (1990), copyright © 1990 Mary Oliver, and 'When Death Comes' from *New and Selected Poems* (Beacon Press, USA, 1992), copyright © 1992 Mary Oliver, by permission of Beacon Press, Boston, and the author, all five poems being published in both *New and Selected Poems* (Beacon Press, USA, 1992) and *Wild Geese: Selected Poems* (Bloodaxe Books, 2004), by permission of Beacon Press and the author. 'West Wind #2' from *West Wind* (Houghton Mifflin, 1997), by permission of Houghton Mifflin Company, this poem also reprinted in *New and Selected Poems: Volume Two* (Beacon Press, 2005).

Molly Peacock: *Original Love* (W.W. Norton & Company, 1995), copyright © 1995 by Molly Peacock, by permission of W.W. Norton & Company, Inc. **Amrita Pritam:** 'Daily Wages', tr. Charles Brasch with Amrita Pritam, first published in *The Penguin Book of Women Poets* (1978), by permission of the Estate of Amrita Pritam.

Rainer Maria Rilke: 'Archaic Torso of Apollo' and 'Buddha in Glory', tr. Stephen Mitchell, from *Ahead of All Parting: The Selected Poetry and Prose of Rainer Maria Rilke*, ed. & tr. Stephen Mitchell (The Modern Library, New York, 1995), copyright © 1995 Stephen Mitchell, by permission of Modern Library a division of Random House, Inc. 'God Speaks to Each of Us', tr. Leonard Cottrell, first published on the Monadnock Review website (20 July 2001), copyright © 2001 by Leonard Cottrell, all rights reserved, by permission of the translator. 'A Walk', 'Sometimes a man' and 'Whoever grasps', tr. Robert Bly, from *Selected Poems of Rainer Maria Rilke, A Translation from the German and Commentary* by Robert Bly, copyright © 1981 Robert Bly, by permission of HarperCollins Publishers. **Rumi:** 'The Guest House', 'Unmarked Boxes', 'Chickpea to Cook' and 'Who Makes These Changes?', tr. Coleman Barks with John Mayne, *The Essential Rumi: Translations* by Coleman Barks (HarperSanFrancisco, USA, 1995; expanded edition, 2004), copyright in both volumes © Coleman Barks, also by kind permission of the Reid Boates Literary Agency. 'Everything You See', tr. Andrew Harvey, *The Mystic Vision: Daily Encounters with the Divine*, ed. Andrew Harvey & Anne Baring (Godsfield Press, Alresford, Hants, 1995). 'A Zero-Circle' from *Say I Am You: Poetry Interspersed with Stories of Rumi and Shams*, tr. John Moyne and Coleman Barks (Maypop Books, 1994), copyright © 1994 Coleman Barks. **Ryokan:** 'In all ten directions of the universe', tr. Stephen Mitchell, from *The Enlightened Heart: An Anthology of Sacred Poetry*, ed. Stephen Mitchell (HarperCollins, USA, 1989; HarperPerennial, 1993), copyright © 1989 Stephen Mitchell, by permission of HarperCollins Publishers.

St John of the Cross: 'Upon a gloomy night', from *Poems of St John of the Cross*, tr. Roy Campbell (Harvill Press, 1951), published by Ad Donker Publishers, an imprint of Jonathan Ball Publishers, Johannesburg & Cape Town. **David Scott:** *Piecing Together* (Bloodaxe Books, 2005). **Shiki:** *The Penguin Book of Zen Poetry*, ed. & tr. by Lucien Stryk & Takahashi Ikemoto (Penguin Books, 1977). **Izumi Shikibu:** *The Ink Dark Moon: Love Poems by Ono no Komachi and Izumu Shikibu, Women of the Ancient Court of Japan*, tr. Jane Hirshfield with Mariko Aratani (Scribner's 1988; Vintage Classics, 1990), copyright © 1990 Jane Hirshfield, by permission of Vintage Books, a division of Random House Inc. **Edith Södergran:** *Complete Poems*, tr. David McDuff (Bloodaxe Books, 1984). **Ernst Stadler:** 'The Saying' from Stephen Berg: *The Steel Cricket: Versions 1958-1997* (Copper Canyon Press, USA, 1997), copyright © 1998 Stephen Berg, by permission of Copper Canyon Press, www.coppercanyonpress.org. **William Stafford:** *The Way It Is: New & Selected Poems* (Graywolf Press, USA,

1998). **Pauline Stainer:** *The Lady & the Hare: New & Selected Poems* (Bloodaxe Books, 2003). **Susan Stewart:** *Columbarium* (University of Chicago Press, 2003), by permission of the author. **Anna Swir:** *Talking to My Body*, tr. Czeslaw Miłosz & Leonard Nathan (Copper Canyon Press, USA, 1996), English translation, copyright © 1996 Czeslaw Miłosz & Leonard Nathan, by the permission of Copper Canyon Press, www.coppercanyonpress.org. **Wisława Szymborska:** 'Four A.M.' from *Poems New & Collected 1957-1997*, tr. Stanislaw Baranczak & Clare Cavanagh (Harcourt Brace & Company, USA, 1998; Faber & Faber, UK, 1999); 'A Little on the Soul', from *Monologue of a Dog*, tr. Clare Cavanagh and Stanislaw Baranczak (Harcourt Trade Publishers, USA, 2006), tr. Clare Cavanagh and Stanislaw Baranczak, © by Wisława Szymborska, 2002, English translation copyright © 2006 by Harcourt Inc., reprinted by permission of the publisher. **Shinkichi Takahashi:** *Triumph of the Sparrow: Zen Poems of Shinkichi Takahashi*, tr. Lucien Stryk with Takashi Ikemoto* (Grove Press, 1986), by permission of Grove/Atlantic, Inc. **R.S. Thomas:** *Collected Poems 1945-1990* (J.M. Dent, 1993), by permission of J.M. Dent & Sons, a division of the Orion Publishing Group Ltd, and Gwydion Thomas. **Jean Toomer:** 'I Sit in My Room', *The Collected Poems of Jean Toomer*, ed. Robert B. Jones & Margery Toomer Latimer (University of North Carolina, Press, 1988), previously unpublished poem from the Jean Toomer Collection, reprinted by permission of the Yale Collection of American Literature, Beinecke Rare Book and Manuscript Library, Yale University. **Tung-shan:** 'If you look for the truth outside yourself', tr. Stephen Mitchell, from from *The Enlightened Heart: An Anthology of Sacred Poetry*, ed. Stephen Mitchell (HarperCollins, USA, 1989; Harper Perennial, 1993), copyright © 1989 by Stephen Mitchell, by permission of HarperCollins Publishers. **Chase Twichell:** *The Snow Watcher* (Ontario Review Press, USA, 1998; Bloodaxe Books, UK, 1999). **César Vallejo:** 'Anger', tr. Thomas Merton, from *Collected Poems of Thomas Merton* (New Directions, 1977), copyright © 1977 by the Trustees of the Merton Legacy trust, by kind permission of Pollinger Limited and the estate of Thomas Merton.

David Wagoner: *Traveling Light: Collected and New Poems (Illinois Poetry Series)* (University of Illinois Press, 1999), copyright © 1999 David Wagoner, by permission of the author and publisher. **Derek Walcott:** *Collected Poems* (1976), by permission of the author and Faber and Faber Ltd. **James Wright:** *Above the River: Complete Poems* (Farrar, Straus & Giroux, Inc., USA, 1990; Bloodaxe Books, 1992), by permission of Wesleyan University Press. **Jay Wright:** *Dimensions of History*, first published by Kayak Books, 1976, © Jay Wright, reprinted in *Transfigurations* (Louisiana State University Press, 2000), © Jay Wright, reprinted by permission of the author.

Al Young: *The Blues Don't Change: New and Selected Poems* (Louisiana State University Press, 1982), copyright © 1982 Al Young, by permission of Louisiana State University Press.

Every effort has been made to trace copyright holders of the poems published in this book. The editors and publisher apologise if any material has been included without permission or without the appropriate acknowledgement, and would be glad to be told of anyone who has not been consulted.

INDEX OF WRITERS

[*translations and notes in italics*]